I AM:

THE BLUEPRINT OF HUMANITY

UNABRIDGED

DAVE HERNANDEZ

FOREWORD BY PETER McHUGH

I AM: The Blueprint of Humanity

Published by:
The JDLD Trust

To contact the author Dave Hernandez by email: dave@hernandez.id.au
Visit: www.iamsonofgod.net

International Standard Book Number:
10:0-9945511-0-X (SC)
13:978-0-9945511-0-8 (SC)

Ebook ISBN:
10:0-9945511-1-8
13:978-0-9945511-1-5

Cover Design: Lisa Hainline, www.lionsgatebookdesign.com
Editing and Interior Book Design: CBM Christian Book Editing
www.christian-book-marketing.com

Printed in the United States of America

ENDORSEMENTS

Dave Hernandez's book, "I AM," is astonishing and influential in its capacity to empower followers of Jesus to live in the fullness of all Jesus became for us and in us. Through an intriguing "story- telling" style, Dave carries his readers into a concise yet, accurate presentation of what, after numerous times of reading the Scriptures, can still appear to be complex and disjointed truths. Truths that help believers in Jesus begin to see and comprehend the extraordinary lengths the Trinitarian God took through love to help restore people into a full and dynamic relationship of being in their family with all the privileges and opportunities of being a son.

Peter McHugh
Senior Minister,
Stairway Church Whitehorse, Melbourne, Australia

==

David Hernandez invites us, with suggested congenial coffee breaks, to join him in a quest for our true identity as humanity, and to discover our own personal "I Am," created in the image of our Creator, the uncreated "I Am."

In this studious, yet poetic work, Dave treads the rich soil of the early Church Fathers as he places the Trinity front and center and presents fresh gleanings of the powerful and purposeful Trinitarian love that first embraced humanity as "family" before the foundation of the world. While human Redemption is the silver thread that he follows through the discourse, he underscores that with the golden thread of Adoption, a subject too often neglected. He awakens the reader to be drawn into the gravitational pull of this Trinitarian belonging and to experience for themselves the "Now Presence" of a loving God and the inner work of "Older Brother," Jesus, in our lives.

The framework of the narrative is presented as two lectures: the first lecture by the first Adam of Genesis, and the second by the last Adam, Jesus Christ of Eternity. While this framework is warm and engaging, the content of their lectures is penetrating and at times even confronting. The author artfully blends framework and content into a humble, but robust challenge to all of us who would seek to know God, and be transformed into our "True Selves" in Him.

I encourage you to pick this book up and have a good read – and don't forget the coffee!

Paul O'Sullivan
Pastor,
Northern Beaches Christian Centre, Mona Vale, Sydney.

Former National chairman of Associated Christian Ministries, Australia.

==

The I AM's of Jesus are common fodder for preachers, but this odyssey by Dave Hernandez is a novel approach to profound truths. Reading it is a liberating experience, opening the way to an exciting renewal of walking with Jesus in the power of the Holy Spirit, the third person of the Trinity so often overlooked and excluded from the church's contemporary teaching. What we believe inevitably affects how we behave, and Dave's odyssey is a timely reminder for us to return to basics, and to live lives that will attract the unbelieving world to Jesus who not only claimed to be, but showed incontrovertibly that He is THE way, THE truth and THE life. Well worth the effort to read, mark, learn and inwardly digest!

Rev David Cohen
Director, Moringa Associates

==

Dave Hernandez's book, "I AM: The Blueprint of Humanity," takes an age-old truth and presents it in a very unique manner, which undoubtedly will help readers see their position in Christ and relationship with the Father in a whole new light. The relationship between God and man, the divine plan and its complexities are dealt with in such a way that the reader can see with fresh understanding the exciting journey ahead of them and a new level of intimacy with the Father, Son and Holy Spirit.

This is not a quick read or a bedtime story, but certainly one to be read. It will help broaden your horizon and possibly bring you into a new place of freedom as you discover your real identity. Take a look into the divine plan, see where you fit, view God's grace and His longing to have an intimate fellowship with the crowning glory of His creation, "man."

Robin Johnson
Co Founder: Beyond Here Inc
Founder: Million Praying Men

==

Dave Hernandez's book, "I AM: The Blueprint of Humanity" is an important book for many reasons. It is a thought-provoking work. It stimulated me to reflect on some critical issues of common Christian belief that need challenging, and it caused me to grow in my appreciation of how good God really is. In the end, whether you agree with everything the author says or not, is irrelevant: the point is that you seriously think about what he is saying.

Using Adam, and then Christ, to be his mouthpieces is an intriguing and original way to communicate a story that has been told many times before. By the end of this book, I had done a lot of highlighting: there are many great thoughts that are worthy of future reflection that will help the reader to comprehend the extraordinary lengths God took to restore humanity to a full and dynamic relationship with Himself and others.

Upon embarking on this adventure, the reader needs to understand that the relatively compact nature of this book does not make it a "quick read." There is definitely some "meat" to chew on, including some of the very well-chosen quotes made at the start of each lecture, and a wealth of information inserted to the footnotes.

Dave makes a valiant effort to explain "the fall" and its consequences, as well as providing the reader with some genuinely good answers to difficult questions that have been poorly dealt with by many evangelical writers and teachers within the Church. I found the "Functions of the Soul" table very helpful for understanding the causes, characteristics, and consequences of both a functional and dysfunctional soul.

Dave is a welcome addition to the growing number of Trinitarian authors who are helping to restore a much-needed understanding to the Church of how unconditional and abundant God's love is for His creation. I hope you will take the time to read, re-read and meditate on "I AM." I can certainly recommend it!

Richard Kerridge
Director, Liberty World Missions

FOREWORD by Peter McHugh

The joy of following Jesus and living in His Kingdom is immeasurable. The freedom promised along with the joy, peace and love are extraordinary. John 17:3, “This is eternal life, that they may know You, the only true God, and Jesus Christ whom You have sent,” declares that we can experience eternal life here, right now as we know through experiences and encounter how marvelous the Trinitarian God is.

Ephesians 3:19 says, “and to know the love of Christ which surpasses knowledge, that you may be filled up to all the fullness of God,” informs us that we are filled up to the fullness of God when what we know by experience and encounter surpasses what we know intellectually. That is, the seat and place of knowledge in our hearts, is more influential than what we know in our heads.

The principal is captured by these verses above is: behavior is always the echo of belief. For example, there is a reason why an individual behaves in anger. Their angry behavior is motivated by something they are believing about their current circumstances. Their angry behavior does not occur in a vacuum or in isolation from what they are believing.

The Apostle Paul understood this truth. His letter to the Romans, Galatians, Ephesians, Philippians and Colossians all begin with what followers of Jesus are to believe about who they became and why, when they accepted by faith the work of His death and resurrection. Having secured right beliefs Paul then describes the behavior that can follow, so that we walk in a manner worthy of our calling. That is, when we believe right we behave right. Consequently, if we don't believe right, we can't behave right.

This is why Dave Hernandez's book, "I AM," is so astonishing and influential in it's capacity to empower followers of Jesus to live in the fullness of all Jesus became for us and in us. Through an intriguing "story telling" style Dave carries his readers into a concise, yet accurate presentation of what, after numerous times of reading the Scriptures, can still appear to be complex and disjointed truths. Truths that help believers in Jesus begin to see and comprehend the extraordinary lengths the Trinitarian God took through love to help restore people into a full and dynamic relationship of being in their family with all the privileges and opportunities of being a son.

In "I AM," Dave Hernandez finds himself being joined to many revelatory authors that the Holy Spirit is raising up in this hour to restore New Testament truths that were lost to religion. Truths that explore the dead works of being "sin conscious" and release the life giving realities of being "son conscious" (Romans 6:11). As the reader takes time to digest and meditate in the truths of "I AM" they will find breakthrough from bondage, a free flow of the rivers of living water that are banked up in their inner being, and overwhelming joy in the new creation realities they will be able to live in.

Peter McHugh
Senior Minister, Stairway Church Whitehorse

Dave Hernandez

PREFACE

I was raised and indoctrinated in a denominational stream that had unique views regarding the Godhead and God's plan of Salvation. The byproduct of their beliefs was a sort of exclusivism that insisted on alienating all people who differ in doctrine. We were saved and those who saw God differently weren't. We lived in fear. If we deviated from the accepted dogmas we would lose our salvation. That fear, combined with a belief that any slipping away from holiness would ban us from God's acceptance, produced in me a mountain of toxic thoughts about myself and God. I lived in guilt and condemnation. I am grateful the leaders and teachers had ingrained in me a love for Scripture and an unshakable faith in God.

Then the unthinkable happened. I fell out of favor. It was one of the most hurtful events in my life. They were my family, and I was banned. But, as I look back today, that event, as hurtful as it was, was one of God's greatest blessings in my life. It drew me closer to God as my Abba, The Spirit as my teacher and Jesus as my Brother.

What followed was incredible. They, Elohim, began to shape me. They started by a total dismantling of everything I was and believed. Slowly they became my family. Father,

Son and Holy Spirit gradually reconstructed me into a Son-of-God.

The process took over 18 years. During that time, I died to everything I was. I found myself in a cocoon. I pushed boundaries. Sometimes I went off on tangents into dead ends. I often moved forward on tiptoes venturing into the unknown. With doubts and hesitations, I moved forward. Slowly I came back to life as They reassembled me, revelation after revelation. God showed me how much I was loved. He removed the guilt and condemnation. Abba taught me Sonship. The Holy Spirit infiltrated deep into the hidden parts of my innermost being, cleansed me by the washing of the Word. Elohim placed within me a clarity that I cannot contain anymore. I have to let the world know the Good News!

This book is the outcome of that process.

My love for God's written Word has grown tremendously. But I cherish even more the gentle harmonies of their Voice in unison speaking the Logos into the depths of my soul. I have my song. I have my voice. This volume is my part in the Symphony of Ages. I hope that as you read these pages, you too, will hear the Voice and find your song.

Here are some thoughts about the book itself:

This book is about a journey that starts in the heart and mind of our Trinitarian-God Creator. It's our adventure, the odyssey of mankind from Adam to Christ. It's a voyage both Adam and Christ propose to take you on. It ventures through the dark places of your fallen condition to the pastures of your risen state in Christ.

It's a recovery expedition into your true identity - the original blueprint of every human being that ever existed. The object is to clear your pathway so you can find that which mankind has lost - the treasure beyond the valley of the Shadow of Death. Sonship in Christ is the treasure to be found. Freedom from shame, lies and fear is our prize. Reflecting the Word into this world is our privilege.

I take on the voices of two main characters who played the most significant roles in the History of Mankind: Adam and Jesus. I do not pretend to speak on their behalf as if I could somehow channel Adam, or prophetically speak as Jesus. It's not my intent. It's more of a role-play than anything else. I only wanted to make a contrast between the two Adams of history and create a more personable content. I pose them as lecturers, guides, each sharing their role in the vast story of man's Redemption, each leading you toward finding the lost bounty.

The book is divided into two parts. The first part is presented by Adam and covers Adam and Eve's creation, their disobedience and its consequences. The second part is presented by Jesus and covers His death and resurrection, through to finding peace in Christ as the Sabbath. I encourage you to take your time as you read each chapter. Look up the footnotes and use a Bible as your main reference. Study each "lecture" until you've assimilated the truths consigned to each paragraph. I am not interested in giving you information and doctrine; I want to accompany you on a journey of restoration and transformation into your original identity in Christ!

I use Abba, Amma and Older Brother to describe the Trinity. This is not a new doctrine; it's not a theology. It is simply a way to describe a family relationship that my wife, children and I enjoy with Elohim. I chose to share that view through Adam because I want you to know this kind of intimacy with them also.

You will also observe (since I am making it obvious by highlighting it now) that I use the term Sons-of-God. It's a significant concept, and I thread it throughout the pages of the book from chapter to chapter. It's the heart of the matter. I do not use the wording "Children of God" nor "Daughters of God." It is not a gender related issue. It's a question of state, identity, who we are! Children: women, and men alike are included as Sons-of-God. I am talking about a people, incorporated as One Body in Christ, and you are invited to join the ever-growing numbers of Sons-of-God releasing God's will on Earth as it is in Heaven.

In Romans, chapter 8, Paul declares:

"For all who are being led by the Spirit of God, these are sons of God." [1] Followed by: *"For the anxious longing of the creation waits eagerly for the revealing of the sons of God."* [2]

Peter writes in his first epistle that, "*You are a chosen race, a royal priesthood, a holy nation, a people for [god's] own possession, so that you may proclaim the excellencies of Him who has called you out of darkness into His marvelous light; for you once were not a people, but now you are the people of god; you had not received mercy, but now you have received mercy."* [3] He describes who we are as Sons-of-God.

I pray you will find your place as a Son-of-God along with the rest of us. I trust you will enjoy the expedition and recover that which is yours!

Love,
Dave Hernandez

ACKNOWLEDGMENTS

I could never thank Elohim enough for taking me on this journey, embracing me and teaching me, correcting me and revealing to me their heart. It honors me to know You and to dwell in your presence.

To my wife, Laurence, who endured the journey and adventure with me from the beginning. Your tenacity and faith inspire me. Your voice is beautiful. I am glad we discovered all this together.

To my two Sons, Damien and Breandan. You never really complained. You followed us through the whole process. You are a gift from God. You taught me fatherhood and drove me to the heart of Abba.

My friend Dale, you were there for a good part of the journey. Your friendship is a gift I hold dear to.

Dave Hernandez

A Word From The Author's Wife

When I started to read Dave's book I couldn't put it down. I knew the journey he'd been on, but now it's a book. It's a marvelous love story between the Creator and His creation; an adventure into the discovery of our origin that brings us back to our Heavenly Family. My prayer for you is that this book will restore your entire being, heal your wounds, mend your hurts and give you hope. I believe it will bring you back to your Heavenly Papa who loves you so much.

For me, meeting my Heavenly Papa brought me to a place where I was accepted by Him the way I was. I didn't need to perform or please Him all the time. He clothed me with a wedding dress and put a crown on my head with colorful diamonds. He taught me to embrace, accept and delight in my whole being: spirit, soul and body. I am His joy, His much-loved daughter, and no law can contravene that truth!

Papa awakened my spirit to Mama Holy Spirit. She gave me all the kindness and tenderness of a real Mum. She opened my ears to Her gentle voice and covered me with Her soft kisses. She is the one I rely on for advice. She wiped away my tears of sadness.

Jesus is my Brother and much more: He is my close friend. Without Him, I would still be lost without knowing who my Heavenly Family is. He's the one who opened the door to Heavenly Places and led me into His glorious and beautiful dwelling. It was a free invitation to become a part again of the family of Heaven. I wasn't an orphan anymore; I was much loved!

As I was in my secret place with Them, I remember my Heavenly Papa breathing on me saying, "We desired you! We made you the way we wanted you to be, and we are pleased."

It's a real honor to serve Elohim and to love Him as He loves me. My story was written at the beginning of the World, and I know that there are more chapters to be lived.

Thank you for this book Dave! I felt honored that you asked me to be one of the first people to read it. I Love you heaps!

Laurence Hernandez

TABLE OF CONTENTS

Part 1: The First Adam

Chapter One

I, Adam

Lecture No 1: I Am God's Creation

"We are not human beings having a spiritual experience. We are spiritual beings having a human experience."

Pierre Teilhard de Chardin

Hi there! I am pleased to meet you. It's great to have you join us for my lecture today. You look familiar; perhaps there is some family resemblance? Of course! Let me introduce myself to you first. I'm you - not exactly you, but the representative and the first of all humanity - I am Adam. As the first of our race, I embody you. I am the representative of our kind since the beginning of history. You were in me, in my loins, when God first created me in bodily form. I carried you in my DNA. I am the first Adam.

I know that I messed things up, but before you judge me, do us a favor: read this book through to the end. I'm not trying to justify myself. I don't need to do that. I just want to clarify a few misconceptions you might have about us. Luckily for us, our Creators knew that we would get things wrong. They had planned a way back home for us all along. I'll get back to the "way-out-of-trouble plan" another time. I just want to put you at ease. Where was I? Oh yes, you existed in me! We also existed in our Creators' thoughts before time and space[4] - the Cosmos[5] - became our realm.

Introducing Our Creators

I didn't witness when our Creators framed the realm in which we would find our physical expression and existence, the first five movements of creation. I came on the scene during the sixth stage. But I walked with them and talked with them, and I got the story first-hand from them. After all, they are the Creators of all things created. These events were recorded for you too, in the book you know as The Holy Bible, God's Holy Word.

Let me talk about our Creators. They are more than just incredible engineers, architects and builders; they are first and foremost a family with an incredible creative bent and more love to give away than you can ever imagine. Creativity and love are embedded in who and what they are. They find joy in us and remain passionately committed to us. We are their love child, the expression of their innermost desire and passion. I remember our times together as if it were yesterday; although it might be a vague concept in your mind; I have never forgotten them. They are Abba, Amma, and Older Brother - at least that's how I call them. They are our originators. You might know them more formally as God the Father, the Holy Spirit and God the Son, but for me, well, I prefer the familiar, informal, family approach.[6] They are family. They are our family. They are Love, Joy, Peace, Wisdom, and everything good you can imagine. They are the perfection of a family. Words are insufficient to truly express who and what they are. I'd hope you'd meet them because knowing them is knowing everything. Had you been there, in the garden, you would know what I'm saying. I know, you were there in me, but it was so long ago and with all the events that have taken place since, it's just become a very distant memory in your consciousness... more like a longing!

Let's not linger too long in this moment of nostalgia, back to our genesis. To simplify my thoughts, I'll refer to Abba, Amma and Older Brother using terminology such as "God," "Elohim"[7], "Yahweh"[8], "The Godhead" or "The Trinity." For me, the term "God" is impersonal, but I'll also use it. Abba, Amma, and Older Brother exist as One God and transcend everything that exists in this Cosmos - they are Elohim. And they exist outside the Cosmos, where there is no time and space. They simply are outside of time, but very present in every moment! They are Yahweh.

Two Realms

One other important thing to know before we unpack the creation story, there are two existential realms that constitute our reality: the first is higher, eternal and exists without beginning and no end: it is the domain of the Creator, the uncreated realm. The second is lower, temporary and exists as a result of Elohim's creative act: the created realm. We'll call this realm the Cosmos.

The Creator's realm is uncreated, of course, and exists outside of the Cosmos. All created things originate in the Creator, from the uncreated realm. This eternal uncreated reality is also known as The Logos. We'll talk more about that in a moment.

Creation is a copy, in physical form, of a superior spiritual reality that finds its origins in God, the Creator. Both realms combined form our reality.

Creation

The Bible starts with these words: *"In the beginning God created the heavens and the earth."* [9] Then it continues its narrative through six periods of creation and a seventh of rest; it reveals that our Creators spoke the universe into existence.

John expands on this idea in the opening statement of his gospel: *"In the beginning was the Word!"*[10] The Logos or "Word" as commonly used in English Bibles, is more than mere words: it is the expression of planned thoughts; logic expressed in spoken words.

God is Love.[11] Abba's, Amma's and Older Brother's plans and logic is love - unconditional love. They speak Their thoughts - thoughts planned as One. The Trinity is indivisible in Word and Love.

Elohim speaks, as One Voice they declare their thoughts; they express their love, and it all becomes visible in the physical form. They said, *"Let there be light,"* and there was light...[12] In each new creation movement they revealed their heart and thoughts in created form. Each new declaration demonstrates a new expression of their heart, mind and desires. Everything they created, our body, this earth, the universe and everything it contains - all the Cosmos - are proclamations of their soul in unison. It is beautiful. Their mind is lovely. Our scientists have barely touched the surface exploring the magnificence of God's thoughts. Many centuries after the creation event, the Apostle Paul explained it this way: *"For since the creation of the world His invisible attributes, His eternal power and divine nature, have been clearly seen, being understood through what has been made."* [13]

Once they had created the heavens and the earth[14] within the Cosmos, they proceeded to create everything we see on planet Earth and then they filled it with every living creature. They looked at every one of their masterpieces of creation and declared with satisfaction: *"It is good!"* [15]

Abba, Amma and Older Brother speak in unison, like a symphonic orchestra - always in harmony - and out of the goodness of their heart and mind their words and love take form and become substance. The Cosmos is their symphony. Their creation is good.

Finally, on the sixth movement of creation, they revealed the pinnacle of their work to both the created and uncreated realms: Us - Me - Adam! We are the greatest revelation of our Originators' heart and mind expressed in the physical form. We are the Chorus of their Symphony. They created the Cosmos for us.

They created us in their image[16] and likeness. We mirror them. We are the "physical resemblance" of a spiritual reality, the reflection on earth of a heavenly substance: God! We are not "God," but we mirror God in the created realm. We model this "likeness" of "Older Brother" the second person of the Trinity.

In his epistle to the church in Colossae, Paul expands on the nature of Older Brother. *"For by Him (Older Brother) all things were created, both in the heavens and on earth, visible and invisible, whether thrones or dominions or rulers or authorities--all things have been created through Him and for Him. He is before all things, and in Him all things hold together."* [17] Older Brother is the model and the purpose of our existence. They created us for Sonship and Rulership.

Sonship

The Apostle Paul writes to the church in Ephesus and explains that, *"God chose us in Him before the foundation of the world, that we would be holy and blameless before Him. In love He predestined us to adoption as sons through Jesus Christ to Himself, according to the kind intention of His will, to the praise of the glory of His grace, which He freely bestowed on us in the Beloved."* [18]

I'm going to explain this passage of Scripture because it's amazing. Abba and Amma wanted us to be a part of their family in Older Brother who is the Eternal Son before they even created the Cosmos. Humanity was always destined to exist in Older Brother. In fact, we were chosen in Him before the foundation of the world. Our physical bodies were created in the likeness of, and to mirror, who we are in Him.

I need to define the term "adoption" at this stage. The Jewish understanding of "adoption" is very different to common western thought. Traditionally, adoption is about accepting a child from another family as your own. The Jewish view is very different. It is the coming into a place of maturity where a son can take on the responsibilities, resources and affairs of his Father.

We have an example of this coming into maturity when John baptized his cousin Jesus. Abba speaks from Heaven, and Amma witnesses the whole scene in the form of a dove. Abba speaks and says, *"You are My beloved Son, in You I am well-pleased."* [19] Jesus' baptism was dramatized as an adoption ceremony. Jesus had come to a place where He was ready to take on the resources and affairs of The Father on earth. This point leads to the Rulership purpose we will uncover next in this chapter. Elohim predestined the whole human race to be adopted Sons-of-God in Jesus Christ, our Older Brother.

God's purpose, since our creation, was always to have mature Sons-of-God rule over Heaven's affairs on Earth! It's always been their motivation. This passage says that God chose us, *". . . according to the kind intention of His will."* In the Greek the words "kind intention" are one word, "eudokia." This word means "good will" and "object of desire and affections." Relationship with Man was the object of God's affections. When Abba declares over Jesus, *"You are My beloved Son, in You I am well-pleased,"* He uses the same word.

The Cosmos is the extension of their thoughts. They created it to give us a physical form in time and space. I, Adam, was fashioned to give a physical expression to spiritual beings. This physical form was designated to reflect spiritual reality. The Trinity had us in them before time, but wanted us to take on a physical form in a created environment for some excellent reasons. Reasons we'll explore throughout these lectures. They created the Cosmos for us and created me, Adam, as the progenitor of Physical Man. However, they - Abba, Amma and Older Brother - are our actual begetters. Older Brother carried the human race in himself in the spiritual just as I carried the physical human race in my DNA. Your physical parents are not the architects of your existence – Elohim is. Your biological parents are honored vessels of, *". . . the kind intentions of His will."*

It may a bit hard to see, I know, but please bear with me awhile, as I develop this further. The reality is the spiritual - the physical is the mirror upon which the spiritual form reflects itself and in which it finds an expression within the created realm. The spiritual is our first nature; the physical is our second nature.

Let me put it another way. The symphony is “set” in Elohim’s heart. The Logos will never vary. The symphony will never be changed or corrupted because it is established for eternity in them. We are their musical instruments, the voices, created to express their melodies in humanity’s history. The Spirit breathes in us, and we become the proclamation of their symphony, the chorus resounding throughout the universe of the music that is forever in their heart. We all have a part in their symphony.

Abba and Amma always wanted to enjoy a close family-like relationship with us as mature Sons. We first exist in Older Brother. We are in them in the uncreated, outside of time, before we take on this physical form. Your biological form is sourced in me, Adam the Physical Man. All for specific reasons we’ll develop throughout this book. The end game however, is for us to enjoy a family relationship with Them in Eternity Future *as* mature adopted Sons in Christ. Time and space (The Cosmos) is but a hiatus in the Eternal “I Am” of our existence.

The Cosmos is a temporary limited place. Older Brother exists in the Eternal NOW of Yahweh - He is the second person of the Trinity. We find our origins in Him; we take our identities from Him; we carry His likeness. And we are destined to spend Eternity Future in Him. Time is a parenthesis in eternity. Elohim had a fail-safe plan to ensure we would be with Them forever. These brackets inserted into eternity provide a safe place for humankind to grow into maturity as Sons-of-God. [20]

While we took on a physical form and expression within this parenthetic insertion, we never stopped existing in spiritual, eternal form - in the Logos - in the Symphony! The spiritual, eternal uncreated realm is our genesis and destiny. Oh, of course, we did lose sight of our origins because of me, but our original identities remained safe in Christ, our Older Brother. He is the protector of the blueprints of our lives. Our parts in the Symphony - the original composition - are secure in Him for you.

Elohim created us for Eternal Sonship. We *are* Sons-of-God. We have a spiritual origin and a physical form (bodies). The spiritual exists in the uncreated realm, and the physical exists in the created realm to reflect and give expression to the spiritual: Two forms in two realms. The two forms - created and uncreated; time and timelessness; reality and mirror - came together when I, Adam, was created. The two dimensions are One reality, our truth. That singularity, the reflection of the spiritual into the physical realm, is me, Adam and us as, “Sons-of-God.”

Sonship in relationship to our Originators is the primary position from which all our purposes in Heaven and the Cosmos take meaning and authority. If our “Sonship” is challenged and undermined, we are lost. I know you might have more questions here, so I promise that I will unpack more about this design in my next lecture.

Rulership

When Elohim created us, they crowned us with glory and majesty and placed us “a little lower than himself.” Then they gave us the mandate to rule over the works of their hands[21]. Mind-blowing when you think about it! Perhaps you can’t imagine what that means, no thanks to me, and I’m not very proud of this, your ability to grasp what I am sharing with you may be somewhat limited. Believe me, God created your brain to perceive things that would dwarf Einstein’s abilities, but unfortunately I messed that up.

Our Creators didn’t create us like they did every other beast on the Earth. As a matter of fact, I spent time acquainting myself with all the animals they had created; giving them identities to see if any were “suitable” as a helper. I couldn’t find any[22].

The word “suitable” means “in front of” or “opposite to.” I could not relate “face to face” to any other animal because none were "like" me. The "likeness" this passage refers to is not just about the biological "similarity" to the beasts I named. No animal enjoyed the peculiar and glorious original design of Man like ours. But there is more to that likeness. We read earlier that I, Adam, was created “in the likeness” of God. I was “like” God but not “like” the animals I named. In giving to the animal kingdom identities, I saw none that I could relate to face-to-face on earth as I could with God in Heaven. No other beast could refer to both the heavenly and the earthly realms as I could. And I couldn’t relate to any animal on earth as I could with God in Heaven.

The Divine Family created us for Sonship and to rule over their creation. They designed us specifically for this purpose. I was not just a son; I was Son-of-God; God’s Priest; a representative of Heaven on Earth. I was a Royal Priesthood. As such I was the only created being, in the Genesis narrative, to be clothed and crowned with glory and majesty. This glory was the Glory of The Son - Our Older Brother - and we shared it with Him. We mirrored His Glory on Earth!

Chapter Two

I, Adam

Lecture No 2: I Am A Soul

> *"Imagination is the beginning of creation.*
> *You imagine what you desire,*
> *you will what you imagine*
> *and at last you create what you will."*
>
> George Bernard Shaw

So, have you followed me so far? A bit hard to grasp?

In my first lecture, we introduced thoughts about our Creators and the ideas that Elohim created us for Sonship and Rulership as Sons-of-God. I want to expand on these ideas in this next lecture. I will also add to my first lecture some thoughts about what it means to have a soul.

Are you ready for this? Relax, grab a cup of coffee - my favorite is double espresso cappuccino - and let's do this.

A Peculiar Design

When our Originators created us, they formed my physical body out of the dust of the Earth. Then they breathed into my nostrils the breath of life, and I became a living being[23].

The original word for "being" means "soul." God breathed into me His "Spirit," and I became a living "Soul." This phenomenon did not happen to the other animals on the planet - that is why I could not find an animal "suitable" to me. None was like me! We will unpack the purpose and function of the soul later on in this lecture. No other created animal in the Genesis narrative experienced what happened to me! We are not mere animals.

First, they formed our physical bodies out of clay. Next they breathed their Spirit of Life into us. God placed eternity in our hearts[24]. God is our source of life. Paul declared: *"In Him we live and move and have our being, ... 'For we also are His offspring.' "*[25]

God created us with a body; He breathed His Spirit into us, and we became a living soul. The body of clay is the tabernacle for God's particular thoughts about you (Logos) to inhabit. I became a living being. I became an "I Am" expression of "The I Am".

We are spirit, soul and body. We are a spiritual being (persona), have a soul and a physical body on Earth to reflect our Heavenly origins in God, The Son. Our physical body is alive by the Spirit of Life breathed into us by God. In his first epistle, John explains this state of being. He writes, *"By this we know that we abide in Him and He in us, because He has given us of His Spirit."* [26] We are in God (The Son), and God (The Spirit) is in us. That's how God created me, Adam.

Then they clothed us with Glory. God breathed into us His Life, and shared with us His Glory and Majesty. We share the Glory of The Son - Older Brother. The Psalmist writes about the Glory in Psalm 8.[27] God crowned us, indeed clothed us, with His Glory. I, Adam was initially covered with Spirit and Glory.

The glory of Older Brother clothed me. That is why Eve and I, *"were naked but we were not ashamed."*[28]

Imagine admiring yourself wearing new clothes in the mirror. You look great! The mirror reflects the reality, but it is you, the one clothed in this outfit that is the real you. The true you is the spiritual person that dwells in Older Brother. It is Older Brother's glorious person that covers you. Our clothing was Heavenly in origin and nature, but visible in the physical realm: the glory of The Son! Eve and I reflected the Glory on Earth that clothed us in Heaven.

Eve

Eve is my wife. I was stunned when Abba brought her to me. You remember when I named all the animals? Well, there were none I could relate to at my level. God had clothed and designed no other animal like He did me. I enjoyed a loving relationship with Abba, Amma and Older Brother. I knew a face-to-face relationship with Elohim in Older Brother. But nobody on Earth was like me. So they put me to sleep and out of me, my rib, Abba, Amma and Older Brother brought forth a stunning "other" version of me. She was a duplicate of me, but separate to me. She was a perfect fit for me, like two pieces of one puzzle. We complimented each other. She was my soulmate, my alter-ego. When Abba introduced her to me I was gobsmacked, dumbfounded. Then and there Abba performed our marriage with Amma and Older Brother as witnesses. And we were One.[29]

Eve and I would relate to each other face to face on Earth just as together we would relate face to face with Abba, Amma and Older Brother in Heaven.

We were madly in love with one another. We knew real love. Pure. Unconditional. Incredible Love. I wish every couple would experience the oneness and love we experienced in each other. It was like she was always a part of me, and I was always a part of her. This experience enabled me to understand how Abba, Amma, and Older Brother relate to each other. They are One Being - Elohim - but each is an extension of each other living in perfect harmony and submission. They share the same Love and are indivisible in Word. That is what marriage *is*: we *are* One.[30] I'll come back to this in a moment, but first, I want to continue the conversation about our design.

Created to Reflect the Supernatural

So, we are a physical body of clay animated by the Spirit of Life. The physical was created to reflect the image of the spiritual persona modeled upon Older Brother in whom we find our genesis. The Spirit dwells in us, and we dwell in Older Brother. The purpose of this body of clay was to enable us to reflect the realities of Heaven and incarnate our unique expression of the Logos on Earth.

Yahweh purposefully designed us with this ability to access Heaven and Earth for many reasons, but one of them was so we could, *"rule over the works of His hands."* [31] Sonship alone does not warrant this design. They could have just placed us in the Heavenly Realm without creating the earthly reflection to enjoy a blissful eternal relationship with us as a beautiful family - although it probably wouldn't have been that simple. Rulership over the created realm does! However, it is important to stress that Rulership flows from Sonship. In other words, if we don't remain in the place of Sonship with God then our attempts at Rulership will be vain. Rulership *is* mature Sonship - that is what adopted Sons are.

The Soul

To understand this peculiar dual-realm design, the purpose and function of the soul need to be further unpacked, so I'm going to delve into some technical talk. Please stick with me and I promise I'll make it as simple as possible to understand. Hopefully.

In my first lecture, I mentioned that Elohim has a heart and mind and that creation was the expression of Their planned thoughts. Elohim is a relational being: a Trinity of three Divine Persons - Abba, Amma and Older Brother - who exist in perfect love, respect, honor and submission to each other. They are distinct Divine Persons, and they are One entity, but their identities are not blurred nor enmeshed. They relate with perfect affection for one another. They *are* Love[32].

Elohim is relational. They are affectionate. Abba, Amma and Older Brother created us with the idea of sharing their thoughts and affections with us: for Sonship.

Relationships are more than just social interactions: healthy relationships include affections, honor and respect. Elohim is not selfish in His affections: He is generously relational and affectionate. Believe me, I know how generous they are. Just take a look at the planet we call home: Elohim generously appointed this world with everything we need. Then, look at the universe. It's all an expression of Their generosity. They didn't put us in a monotonous box. This realm mirrors their domain and heart.

God has a soul. The soul is the seat of the heart (emotions), mind (thoughts) and affections (relationships). Our affections were designed to be fulfilled in relationship with the Trinity first and one another as a flow on effect.[33] The soul is the place where emotions, thoughts and affections are processed and find meaning. The three functions combined are the Logos. When the Logos is expressed, they act and create. Yahweh has a heart, a mind and is relational. He speaks and creates all things from the overflow of His soul. This process is the exercise of the will! The will executes what the soul has planned. James says, *"In the exercise of His will God brought us forth by the word of truth!"* [34]

When Elohim breathed into my nostrils, He imparted to me the functions of His very own soul: the abilities to think, feel and relate which combined enable us to create. Amazing! Our souls mirror Elohim's soul. But not only did He impart to me the same functions, He imparted to me Their thoughts. This includes thoughts and plans about me and about His will for me and all of creation.

Their symphony - my part in the song of Ages - is in me; it is indeed who I am. I have my song to sing in their Universal Choir - I am my voice echoing their voice. Christ is the keeper of the original sheet music!

They said, *"Let Us make man in Our image, according to Our likeness; and let them rule..."* [35] They gave me a body to reflect The Son, and they gave me a soul to mirror Their Soul. This design enabled me to remain aware of everything that was happening around me in both the Spiritual and the Physical realms. I was able to relate to the uncreated realm and the created realm at the same time. In other words, I could relate to both Heaven and Earth all the time reflecting upon Earth the reality of Heaven.

God's Grand Design

God designed us to relate to Him as our Father and to rule over the works of His hands. The physical body receives information from the created realm. We can see, hear, taste, touch and smell. The senses give us an awareness of the physical realities around us. In the same token, our spiritual personas enjoy similar functions: the ability to remain aware of what is happening in Heaven in and through the Son. If the physical body becomes impaired, we lose awareness and the ability to function well in the physical realm. Likewise with the spiritual, if our link to the spiritual realm is damaged, we lose all our spiritual awareness and functionality.

As I said earlier, I botched things up and I messed up big time! I severed the link with the Heavenly Realm; I created a veil. I will talk some more about this in other lectures, but first I want you to understand this unique design of ours.

The soul is like a "device" that processes the information it receives from both physical and spiritual realms. The soul is a bridge between Heaven and Earth. We process information in three stages: relationally, emotionally and rationally, sometimes going around in circles. The outcome of this process triggers the enactment of our will: we create our realities. Just as God created the universe from what was in his heart and mind, we create our world. I need to add that each soul is tuned according to their unique part in the song. You will always process the signals and information according to your personal tuning.

In my original design, I always remained aware of Heaven *and* Earth. Heaven was my primary source of truth, love and affection. I was aware of God's will to reflect it on Earth. When I did that, my soul would release Heaven's realities on Earth in line with humanity's mandate and my unique tuning.

My knowledge, instructions, acceptance and affections were sourced from Heaven first, and then I would process it all in my soul and live it out on Earth. I saw God's will fulfilled on Earth as it was in Heaven. And it all happened through me - reflected by me! It was all an act of my will.

You see, God designed us to rule over His created realm. I, Adam, was God's Ambassador. I was God's Priest. I was God's Prime Minister. And so I had access to God's Throne anytime I needed to as Son and Ruler. I could walk in and out of the Throne Room of Heaven at my will. God created us this way for that purpose! This access, in and out of the Heavenly, was made possible in Older Brother, the second Person of The Trinity. He is our gateway into the Heavenly[36] and will always remain as such throughout time.

Chapter Three

I, Adam

Lecture No 3: **I Am Holy**

"Our deepest fear is not that we are inadequate.
Our deepest fear is that we
are powerful beyond measure.
It is our light,
not our darkness that most frightens us."

Marianne Williamson
from her book "A Return To Love"

Well, so far we've established a foundation upon which we'll continue to build on. In my first two lectures, I determined that we were created with equal access to Heaven and Earth because we are Sons-of-God called to rule over the works of God's hands. God gave us a soul to mirror His own, so we could do His will on Earth as it is in Heaven.

Ready for more? Another double-shot-cappuccino perhaps? A doughnut with that?

Let's do this!

Holiness

This unique "dual-realm" design reveals a particular fact about us: we are Holy - Man is Holy. I'll try not to be too boring here, but I need to define holiness - in my opinion there have been too many misconceptions about this word.

There are three main ideas combined that define what is Holy (the concept of Holiness): clean, unique and set aside. I want to spend a little bit of time exploring these three ideas.

The word "clean" means pure, undefiled, not corrupted, uncontaminated, untainted, unpolluted, free (from dirt, corruption, foul matter), immaculate, perfect, and intact. God created me, Adam, undefiled by any lies, fear and evil. I was perfect; not just a sight for sore eyes - I was quite handsome in my prime - the perfection I'm talking about is that I was untainted by anything evil. I was free. Free indeed!

The word "unique" means uncommon, not ordinary, incomparable, totally other, rare, distinct, inimitable, matchless, unrivalled and without equal. No other created being could compare to Eve and I. We were unique by virtue of creation and nature.

The concept of being "set aside" points to ideas such as sacred, sanctified, set apart, made holy, reserved, kept, chosen, selected, elected. Yahweh sanctified us unto Himself and gave us a unique design for a particular purpose. I, Adam, was Holy by design, purpose, and I was pure and truly free.

We are a unique being by design for the purpose of Sonship and Rulership. As such, we are Holy! Holiness encompasses our identity and destiny. Even after I messed it all up - we never stopped being Holy in God's eyes. That's why He made sure we would recover our true selves and unique voices. The Son-of-God protected the blueprints of our identities since before I ever sinned, even before the foundation of the Cosmos!

As I said before, I blew it, and I take responsibility for it. I sinned and consequently you are a sinner in me. Holiness, however, is not a pursuit to become sinless; it is a fact one discovers in the recovery of one's original uniqueness. We never lost this holiness - we lost "sight" of it when darkness shrouded our world because of our disobedience. The sheet music of your song has never been lost and cannot be corrupted; you just stopped singing and are out of tune.

The understanding of holiness affects one's behavior. God called me to represent Him. God designed me to enjoy a privileged relationship with Himself. God inscribed the understanding of my sacredness in my heart. He embedded holiness into our identity as Sons-of-God.[37]

Paul commands the church in Ephesus to, *". . . put on the new self, which in the likeness of God has been created in righteousness and holiness of the truth."*[38] The "new self," as we will explore throughout these lectures, is the reality I enjoyed before the fall as Son-of-God. It's the Heavenly Persona in Christ reflected upon Earth. It's the Son-of-God created in Christ's likeness in righteousness and holiness that we, humans, have lost sight of! The "new" self is the you Jesus redeemed on the cross and revealed in the resurrection! It's the true you that Christ protected in Himself as the Lamb-of-God who was slain before the Cosmos was framed[39]. There's never really been a new song - it's the original song discovered by you. What I lost because of my disobedience Jesus redeemed, preserved and revealed because of His obedience.

Our bodies of clay are tabernacles for the Logos - God's particular thoughts and affections about you. What God envisaged for you exists first and always in Him in Logos form. Then it is imparted to you as a unique "I am" representative of "The I Am." The Lamb's Book-of-Life is the Logos preserved and protected throughout time in Christ, The Lamb. It's the original sheet music of their symphonic composition. Christ secured our original innocence and identity. He holds the blueprints of our lives and they have remained unscathed in Him, in His Book-of-Life! Humanity remains Holy in Christ! Jesus became the Logos-made-Flesh to demonstrate to us our original Holiness in Him!

In Jesus, the full spectrum of our original Holiness is shown to us. Christ retained this Christ-Identity (you in Christ) in its original Holiness, including your freedom and sinlessness. One cannot create this Holiness through effort or following formulas. Self-sanctification is impossible.[40] Building our identities through self-effort has proven itself a disaster: that's what Eve and I attempted in the first place.

Members of the Royal Family do not try to become "Royals." They live out of understanding and embracing their royalty. Their identity affects their behavior. They act in agreement with the ways of royalty, not to become Royals, but because of whom they are.

I lost all that, but Jesus recovers and redeems it all. I wish you would all wake up to this astonishing reality, so you could all live in the fullness of Sonship.

You cannot become sinless through works; there's no way you can undo what I did. Jesus already did that. However, you need to recover the vision of "whom we are." That's why I'm reaching out to you now. If you could understand your holiness, then everything would change in this world.

I'm getting ahead of myself again. That's because I'm so excited about what Jesus did as Older Brother. He had done it all before I disobeyed. Oh, that doesn't mean I don't understand what I did as the first Man, but what He did was far greater and I just want you all to know it. And to think that He was there all along for us!

The whole meaning of life stems from the revelation that we are Holy among all creation because we are Sons-of-God. Everything else flows from that!

Identity

I think I might have said this before - forgive me if I seem to repeat myself - but the process I went through to understand my identity was interesting. I had to figure out that there were no other created beings I could relate to "face to face" and through that process I realized what I was not. I realized that I was not a lion, a monkey or a snake: I was Man. I am Adam. I am unique: Holy. I, Adam am Son-of-God. That was my defining moment. Adam means Man. I am Adam by name and Man as a sacred species of God's creation. This discovery was important for me. At that moment, I found my place and purpose in the order of nature. God created me a little lower than Himself, and to rule the created realm including all living animals.

Naming (calling forth and shaping one's identity) is a divinely appointed role given to Fathers. Throughout Scripture, we see fathers name their sons. I was given the job to name the animals not only to define my identity as Son-of-God, but so I could rule over the works of God's hands as a father would.[41] As did Abba with humanity! I attributed to each species their place and purpose in the animal Kingdom.

Abba blessed us with our identities. He blessed everyone with a unique identity. He gave us all a name and wrote it in the Lamb's Book-of-Life. Jesus was the Lamb-of-God slain before the foundation of the world. [42] The Lamb-of-God was slain to protect every Identity throughout all history - the names written in the Book-of-Life. Elohim consigned the names of every person that will ever exist to that Book - in His Son - since before time began. The timelessness of

Christ as the Lamb-of-God, who was slain before we, humanity, sinned in me (Adam) is a foundational truth. Although Jesus walked among us 2000 years ago, the actual slaying was done before sin occurred. Christ's physical visitation, death, burial and resurrection was an announcement to the world to commemorate what had already happened at the beginning of time. It turned a spiritual event that occurred before time into an actual official historical event that took place in time and space. The timing of Jesus' coming among us was right because this truth and event needed to be witnessed, recorded for the ages and broadcasted at large. No other time in history was more favorable for the sacramentalisation[43] of the Son's sacrifice to take place. Every life that will ever live in the Adamic likeness is ordained and blessed by God before time began. That blessed identity remained protected in Older Brother throughout our history. When God created me, Adam, He blessed me. When He blessed me, He blessed you in me. Your identities, however, were not kept in me; They originate and are held in Christ for the right time in history. Jesus' death as the Lamb-of-God was a preemptive and protective act.

Your coming into history is a sacramental act that broadcasts into time and space an event that took place before creation: your coming into being in Older Brother!

Psalms 139 says: *"You place your hand of blessing on my head."* [44] followed by, *"Every day of my life was recorded in your book. Every moment was laid out before a single day had passed. How precious are your thoughts about me, O God!"* [45]

Of course, this Psalm refers to the person who lives as a Son-of-God in the original purposes of God's design for humanity - in that place of unconditional love. But remember, when God first created us, that's who and what we were: Sons-of-God, a Holy people. Elohim blessed us at creation. And then we must also remember that Christ, the Lamb of God, preserved our original design and purpose in Himself. Christ saw the unique you when He died for you because you were in Him! His purpose was to connect you with everything you are in Him since the foundation of the Earth through His resurrection. You are saved to live in that unique and blessed identity and purpose Christ kept in Himself for you.

My disobedience caused us all to lose sight of who we are in Christ. Since then we've been searching for our identities. The search for identity is, in fact, a search for Holiness. When one seeks to "stand out," to be "different," one is seeking an identity. I see you do that all the time. I see it in how you chose your clothes and your status updates on Facebook. I see it in the car you drive and the house you buy. You are constantly trying to establish your point of difference - a uniqueness - something that will set you apart from the crowd. In reality, you seek Holiness. The point you miss is that it is our Creators who set us apart, and they create us uniquely for their purposes.

Let me suggest in closing this lecture that since the fall, Mankind, generally speaking, has still yet to discover its' identity. As a corporate body, we still don't know what we're not (like all the other animals) as opposed to what we are (Sons-of-God). We are still in the early stages of understanding our identity in the scope of God's overall plan.

Goodness, did I mess things up!

Chapter Four

I, Adam

Lecture No 4: I Am A Free Moral Agent

"Love is the only reality and it is not a mere sentiment. It is the ultimate truth that lies at the heart of creation."

Rabindranath Tagore

Is your head spinning yet? Quite a lot to take in right? I hope you've taken the time to rest since my last lecture. Had some lunch maybe? If you're back, you're obviously ready for another talk. So let's get on with it.

Let's review the key ideas from our previous lectures first. Six big ideas have emerged:

1. God created us for Sonship and Rulership;

2. God designed us to relate to both the created and uncreated realms;

3. The physical mirrors the spiritual. Our physical bodies reflect our spiritual personas. The spiritual is the substance; the physical is a mere reflection of the spiritual.

4. God is the originator and architect of our identities. Abba and Amma are the progenitors of our spiritual personas. We are the expression of the Trinity's love. Older Brother carried and protected us in Himself; I, Adam bore your DNA in myself; I am the progenitor of your physical bodies.

5. Our soul is designed to process information and act in such a way that the will and way of Heaven become the reality on Earth.

6. We are Holy beings because God uniquely designed us among all creation, and set us apart for a unique purpose, we remained untainted by evil in Christ.

God created us entirely free (until, of course, Eve and I blew it - you don't need to keep reminding me of that do you?).

In this lecture, I want to unpack the idea of free moral agency.

Unconditional Love

God created me and therefore us, with the idea of sharing His affections and thoughts with us, to enjoy a perfect Father-Son relationship.

God practices pure, unconditional, uncontaminated and unrestricted love. God is love.[46] Love is from God.[47] I know that because that's how Abba, Amma and Older Brother have always related to me. Eve and I would walk with them in the garden every evening[48].

Back then, we all lived in perfect love and shared pure affections for one another. That is all I knew. Abba, Amma and Older Brother shared that love with me. I shared that love with Eve. Eve and I were at one with God because of love. This scripture describes the perfect relationship I shared with the Divine Family before our disobedience: *"God is love, and the one who abides in love abides in God, and God abides in him."*[49]

Without knowing Elohim, we cannot know the fullness of unconditional love. I knew and lived in that love. Today, however, because of my disobedience, you can only define love through darkened sunglasses. You can only express and know that kind of love in part. In his famous chapter on love, the Apostle Paul puts it this way: *"Now we see things imperfectly as in a poor mirror, but then we will see everything with perfect clarity. All that I know now is partial and incomplete, but then I will know everything completely, just as God knows me now."* [50] We need a full restoration of our sight to know the depth, width and breadth of pure unconditional love and to know ourselves as God knows us.

Obedience

Obedience is the outworking of being in agreement in a partnership of love. Obedience is easy when love motivates it. I had no problems obeying God when everything Eve and I did was motivated and understood in an environment of perfect, unconditional love.

When we agree with God - as Eve and I did - the outworking is powerful and beautiful. Love was the driving force. Eve and I walked with Yahweh and were in total agreement with Him. We ruled over the works of Elohim's hands as an act of obedience to a commandment that they had spoken in the form of a blessing. God says, *"Be fruitful and multiply, and fill the earth, and subdue it; and rule over the fish of the sea and over the birds of the sky and over every living thing that moves on the earth."* [51]

Uncontaminated Truth

Truth is the building block for relationships and purity of affections (unconditional love) is the mortar; together they create a house of freedom and trust. Eve and I knew we were unconditionally loved. We also knew that God would only speak truthfully and honestly to us. We knew that everything that preceded out of Abba's, Amma's and Older Brother's mouth was nothing but Truth - their perfect thoughts.

The Evangelist John explains that, *"The Word became flesh, and dwelt among us, and we saw His glory, glory as of the only begotten from the Father, full of grace and truth."* [52] Truth has its source in Heaven, from the heart of God. God speaks and it becomes visible. God cannot lie; it is impossible for him to lie[53] because He is Truth. Jesus says: *"You will know the truth, and the truth will make you free."* [54] Theirs is a house of liberty. Keeping our thoughts aligned with their thoughts is the essence of obedience.

In that environment of truth and love, we enjoyed freedom and trust. Trust was mutual. We communicated truthfulness in both directions. Love meant we knew they had our best interest at heart and would never put us in harms way. Truth and trust allowed us to act freely upon our wills in total agreement with God, without coercion and manipulation. In that environment, we could speak freely. We worked with God, in accord and not under compulsion. God never manipulated us and always ensured we could make informed decisions. They respected us. They honored us. Eve and I respected, esteemed and loved them with every breath we had.

God-Blessed Identity

The third factor that weighs in heavily on decision-making is the issue of blessed identity - Holiness. We were blessed and understood our holiness. We knew that we were Sons-of-God. We were also in tune with our unique voices.

We knew perfect love, pure truth and understood our holiness. The three combined in Christ are Logos: God's planned thoughts for and about us. The outcome of living in The Logos was that obedience was never a problem. Not until ... well, you know.

The Will

So, having established a framework for understanding how obedience works, let's go deeper. Obedience is the act of the will. God created us with an incredibly glorious purpose, but He did not create us to be machines. At creation we enjoyed free will - we were free moral agents.

We process our wills through our emotions, thoughts and affections. Say, for instance, you meet a complete stranger and ask him to wash your car on Saturday morning. He would first process your request through the grid of relationship and since you are a stranger. He would decide that the appropriate response is, "You do it!" Your relationship to this man determined the response. However, if you were to ask your son the same thing, what would his response be? He would process the request emotionally, and the usual response is, "I do not feel like it, Dad!" There's no rational reason here, just an emotional response. With added incentive on your part, your son adds reasoning to the process. He decides that complying is the appropriate choice. He agrees and then acts according to his will. He enacted upon his will as the result of processing a request through the grids of relationship, emotions and thoughts. Of course, things get more complicated than that but, in a nutshell, to be a free moral agent means we are free to process information, to formulate an appropriate response and then to act.

The factors that enable me to make right decisions are these:

- I know who I am and I know who you are in relationship to me;
- I understand all the ins and outs of my decision;

- I feel free about my decision because I am loved and I am not coerced nor manipulated.

When God acts upon His will, He speaks and creates the universe we see. Likewise, man's will creates His world from what is within his soul. God did not expect me, Adam, to fulfill my responsibilities mindlessly. God empowered me. Elohim wanted me to use my will to carry out their will. It means that nothing could harm the relationship in any way: truth, love and honor (a sense of blessed identity) had to be protected at all cost.

The Harmonious Soul

A soul immersed in The Logos – as Eve and I knew before our disobedience – works in perfect harmony and the outcome is blessed. Each function of the soul is "covered" or "crowned" by a ruling value.

Paul's writings to the church Colossae encourage the saints in this way:

"So, as those who have been chosen of God, holy and beloved, put on a heart of compassion, kindness, humility, gentleness and patience; bearing with one another, and forgiving each other, whoever has a complaint against anyone; just as the Lord forgave you, so also should you. Beyond all these things put on love, which is the perfect bond of unity. Let the peace of Christ rule in your hearts, to

which indeed you were called in one body; and be thankful. Let the word of Christ richly dwell within you, with all wisdom, teaching and admonishing one another with psalms and hymns and spiritual songs, singing with thankfulness in your hearts to God. Whatever you do in word or deed, do all in the name of the Lord Jesus, giving thanks through Him to God the Father." [55]

Peace rules our hearts (emotions). Paul says to the Colossians: *"Beyond all these things put on love, which is the perfect bond of unity. Let the peace of Christ rule in your hearts, to which indeed you were called in one body; and be thankful."* [56] The *"peace of God, which surpasses all comprehension"*[57] covers the heart. Peace is the outworking of love.

Wisdom rules our minds (intellect). Colossians 3 says, *"Let the word of Christ richly dwell within you, with all wisdom teaching and admonishing one another with psalms and hymns and spiritual songs, singing with thankfulness in your hearts to God."* [58] The wise man says, *"The fear of the LORD is the beginning of wisdom, And the knowledge of the Holy One is understanding."* [59] Without wisdom, every form of information we store up and process in our minds (such as logic, common sense, facts, and data, or ideological and philosophical thinking, etc.) is useless. Proverbs says, *"He who gets wisdom loves his own soul."* [60] Wisdom is the outworking of perfect truth. The author of Proverbs 21 declares, *"He who pursues righteousness and loyalty finds life, righteousness and honor."* [61] Honor is the expression of a blessed identity.

Honor rules relationships (our affections). To honor is to prefer others before oneself and to recognize the intrinsic value of others. Paul says, *"So, as those who have been chosen of God, holy and beloved, put on a heart of compassion, kindness, humility, gentleness and patience; bearing with one another, and forgiving each other, whoever has a complaint against anyone; just as the Lord forgave you, so also should you."* [62]

The three elements working in harmony are a hallmark of a soul working in agreement with Heaven and living immersed in The Logos - Elohim's thoughts about us and for us: their perfect plans. [63] That's how I carried out God's will on Earth as it is in Heaven. My soul was in harmony with God's. Eve and I lived in wholeness. We mirrored the reality of Heaven. A soul that is in harmony sings in tune with Heaven's symphony!

The three overarching values affect each other and create balance. Prosperity flows from such a soul. John writes In his third Epistle, *"Beloved, I pray that in all respects you may prosper and be in good health, just as your soul prospers."* [64] When one acts in agreement with God with a pure (uncorrupted) soul one's decisions will always produce life, blessings, and prosperity. In summary, I have put it all together in table format. I find it gives a great overview of the concepts I've presented so far and it also adds some extra ideas. I feel this table makes sense of it all.

"Parts" of The Soul	**Functions of The Soul**	**Functional Soul in Relationship with God**	
		Divine Input: Logos	**Harmonious Output: "Ruling Values"**
Heart	Emotional	Unconditional **Love**	Peace
Mind	Rational	Uncontaminated **Truth**	Wisdom
Affections	Relational	God-Blessed **Identity**	Honor
The WILL as outcome of processing our thoughts, emotions and affections		My Will is in Harmony with God's Will = Free Will (Freedom)	A Prosperous Soul = Prosperous Lifestyle & Healthy Body

When the soul functions in the way God created it to function - bathed in the Logos - it receives "input" from God through the Spirit (unconditional love, uncontaminated truth and God-blessed identity rule). In that state, Man can act upon his will in agreement with Heaven's will in total freedom, confidence and a healthy sense of security. The outcome is a prosperous lifestyle, meaningful relationships, and healthy body ruled by peace, wisdom and honor. These traits will be evident, like fruit on a healthy tree.

The physical life we live on Earth is a reflection of God's thoughts (Logos) spoken into our spiritual personas and processed through our souls. That can be true, of course, only when the spirit is alive!

Eve and I lived this way before the fall. Although, to be honest, we were a bit out of tune with Heaven's pitch due to our immaturity.[65] Jesus enjoyed this lifestyle all His life.

I want to conclude this lecture with one final word. To be a free moral agent means we operate freely in an environment with relationships as described above. It means our souls are free to process everything that comes in (input) without corruption. The whole process must remain free of contaminants, so to speak. I would suggest that any form of "impairment" to the soul would result in denying the free moral agent the ability to act freely. It doesn't mean you lost your freedom; it means you have lost control of the outcome of your choices because your ability to chose without fear, lies and shame is impaired. Corruption would mean that the free moral agency is lost. We, Eve and I, corrupted your ability to act as free moral agents when we disobeyed God. Since our disobedience, our decisions have been ill-informed because our hearts, minds and affections were impaired and therefore we, the human race, have made many destructive choices. In many cases, and without trying to absolve us of our responsibilities, I would say that we acted without choice. It was imperative therefore that Jesus, Mankind's Redeemer, would seek to restore the fullness of our freedom to act as free moral agents.

Chapter Five

I, Adam

Lecture No 5: I Am Immature

"All men make mistakes,

but only wise men

learn from their mistakes."

Winston Churchill

Ready for another session? I guess we better get on with it then!

In this lecture, I want to begin to discuss a very sensitive event in our history. You guessed it! My disobedience.

The Need To Mature

Two men came into this world in a state of perfection enjoying wholeness, peace and harmony. They were me - The first Adam - of course, and Jesus - The last Adam. [66] We did not need to seek perfect love, uncontaminated truth, and a blessed identity: we enjoyed those things as naturally as we breathe air. As such, our ability to make informed decisions as free moral agents was uninhibited. We enjoyed blessedness, but even blessed identities need to mature. Eve and I were created perfect and unblemished, but we *were* immature and we needed tuning.

Imagine the best family environment where children experience unconditional love, truth, honesty and blessings. It could be your family. You speak blessings over your kids, encourage them, show love, tell them that you are proud of them, teach them, point out their talents and speak prophetically over their lives. They are blessed! However, you would agree with me, it is through a process of self-discovery and awareness that they will mature into the fullness of their identities. This process will help them discover their unique gifts and abilities, call and destinies. Children are not fully mature in their identities at the age of eight, but can enjoy their blessedness from birth. They are blessed, but not mature.

My process into maturity started in the Garden of Eden before the Fall. I discovered that I was not like any of the other animals in the Garden. However, as “Man” blessed of God, Holy amongst God’s Creation, I still needed to mature into the fullness of my Identity; as did Jesus, the Son-of-Man[67].

Aligning our thoughts (mind, heart and affections) with The Logos leads to maturity. Maturity is also the coming of “being” - the ability to live in the “I am” will of God in perfect reflection of “The I Am.” Although God created Eve and me “gloriously” we were not created mature. We needed to develop into our adoption. These three functions of the soul required to be tuned to reflect the will of God perfectly. My thoughts needed to incarnate God’s thoughts: The Logos. My mind, my heart and my affections needed some tuning. God gave me total freedom in the process.

It is interesting to read that Jesus was perfected[68] through His suffering. Eve and I also needed perfecting. Elohim accompanies us into maturity as we face opposition.

We were immature in the exercise of our wills: we enjoyed a blessed identity, but had not come to enjoy the full maturity of our beings. Although I was a son, I was not a mature Son-of-God!

Remember that the exercise of the will is the result of how we think, feel and relate to our environment. **The alignment of our thoughts, feelings and affections with the Logos (Truth, Love and our Blessed Identities) produces maturity, as we exercise our wills**.

God created us as free moral agents. He gave us a soul in the image of His own by which we can exercise our very own will! The exercise of our will over time defines us. If we use our will in obedience to our Creators' will, our original identity in Christ is being affirmed. If we use our will in disobedience, the process becomes trickier and painful. The opportunity to obey God's commandments determines *how* we mature as Sons-of-God. God's commandments are the expressions of His thoughts to be carried out through the act of our (Man's) will.

Jesus Matured Through Obedience

Jesus, our Older Brother, also known as the Second Adam, matured in His identity. However, he did not do so in opposition to The Father, but did so in obedience: *"Although He was a Son, He learned obedience from the things which He suffered. And having been made perfect, He became to all those who obey Him the source of eternal salvation."* [69]

Jesus proved that we could make decisions in total submission to our Creators' will and remain empowered individuals. He says, *"No one takes my life from me, but I lay it down of my own accord. I have authority to lay it down and authority to take it up again. This command I received from my Father."* [70] Jesus remained in control of His will by doing The Father's will in total freedom. Jesus matured in His identity through obedience. We learn through obedience or disobedience; either is our choice.

Did God's Plan Go Wrong?

The question I want to tackle now is this one: Did God's plan go wrong when Eve and I disobeyed? I know I have to tread carefully here because one might believe I am trying to justify myself. I am not. I am attempting to set the record straight and to present honest answers to age-old questions.

Let's start with two questions.

Question 1: Does God make mistakes? Clearly, the answer must be that God doesn't. There are no design flaws in the way they engineered creation and nature. The universe functions exactly the way they designed it to. We do too.

Question 2: What was God's eternal purpose? Well, we've answered that in previous lectures. Their motivation is love and family. They want us to be in the family forever and to take over the family business as mature Sons without being coerced, nor manipulated. Our eternity with Elohim relies on our personal desire and will.

The answers to these questions must become a guideline to answering the one about my disobedience. If God doesn't make mistakes, then my disobedience didn't surprise them. If adopted Sonship is their purpose, then my disobedience should not distract from that purpose. God knew we needed to mature - to align our thoughts, emotions and affections with Heaven through the exercising of our will.

High Risk

The belief that God's "Plan A" went wrong because we disobeyed would be to accept that God does things by trial and error. God never had a "Plan B." Eve and I acted how God created us to - in freedom - and when one creates a free moral agent there is always a high risk of disobedience leading to dissociation! Unconditional love cannot exist outside of freedom. One cannot enjoy true love if one is coerced and forced to comply.

There is always a probability that the free moral agent will determine whether or not it is indeed free by making a decision contrary to the will of the one who gave free choice in the first place. Abba, Amma and Older Brother knew the odds and were ready to take the risk. They had no choice but to take the risk because love doesn't know any other way.

I was thinking clearly; God did not trick us. They made everything clear to me. *"From any tree of the garden you may eat freely; but from the tree of the knowledge of good and evil you shall not eat, for in the day that you eat from it you will surely die."*[71]

At that moment, I was given the opportunity to exercise my will - not by simply doing what I *was told* to do, but by doing what I *chose* to do. I knew and understood the consequences of my decisions because my soul was not polluted. I hadn't disobeyed yet. I clearly understood the ramifications. The choice I made was as a free moral agent.

Now things get interesting. The thought of disobeying was tantalizing to Eve and I; we would know if we are truly free only if we partook of the forbidden tree. Until this moment, we had always agreed with God. So the thoughts that nagged us were, "Are we obeying because we don't know any other way and are we truly exercising our will?"

The other question was, "How do we know we are truly loved unconditionally if we always do what they expect us to?" I admit the thought process made me feel uncomfortable at first. But slowly we began to consider the options.

Notice where the struggle took place - in our thoughts. Our mindset (pronoia[72]) and thinking that led us to exercise our will were out of line. That's immaturity! A mindset that is not in line with God's original thoughts (Logos) about us can lead to paranoia, which is exactly what happened to Eve and I in regards to God. Our thoughts weren't completely in line with Elohim's thoughts and plans. We can use the word "thoughts" to summarize the process of self-will that incorporates rational thinking along with our emotions and affections. The "mindset" includes the three functions of the soul.

We needed to mature! We had a song, but we needed to tune ourselves to Heaven's pitch.

Risk Elimination

Their Plan A always incorporated our redemption. That's why Older Brother is the Lamb-of-God that was slain before we ever disobeyed. He was slain because I would sin and to protect the blueprints of our lives. This plan was brilliant. Imagine the devastating effects if they had entrusted the original personas of all humanity to me, Adam? Instead, they entrusted the spiritual blueprints of our identities to God-the-Son. I had the responsibility to carry you in me physically. Christ took on the responsibility to protect your innocence and authority. The physical is merely the reflection of the spiritual. My disobedience never affected your original innocent self in Christ; but it did, however, affect the Adamic you. Your spiritual innocence has always been *"hidden with Christ in God"*[73] because Christ *is* our life![74]

Again, you might say to me, "Adam, you are just trying to justify yourself because you made the wrong choice." Believe me I am not. I certainly could have made the right choice and saved us a lot of troubles. It doesn't mean Elohim wasn't more than aware of the probabilities this would go negative; they were more than prepared for that. Nobody undertakes a risky enterprise without an appropriate risk elimination plan! We are too precious in their sight for them to take a chance, see us fail and then discard us.

Free Moral Agents

The free moral agent will seek the empowerment of self as a unique individual, the establishment of identity through the exercise of self-will. The risk is in the immature mind that hasn't learned wisdom. Wisdom is the outworking of the maturing process as we align our thoughts to the Logos.

A child discovers self-will by making choices. Mum says to her little boy, “Don’t touch the oven because it is hot, and it will burn you.” The child smiles and reaches out to the oven and burns himself. The child has discovered what mum meant. This behavior is not sinful nature – it is the instincts of a free moral agent that is at work. The child is gaining understanding and will align his thinking with mum’s. It is possible for a child to make right choices through obedience, but there is a greater probability (aggravated in a fallen environment) that it will learn through disobedience. And because of my original sin our environment is far from perfect, our souls have been corrupted and, therefore, our choices impaired. This fact doesn’t mean we’ve lost the instincts of the free moral agent though.

Winston Churchill said, “All men make mistakes, but only wise men learn from their mistakes.” But another quote - author unknown - says, “Wise men learn from their mistakes, but wiser men learn from the mistakes of others.”

Repentance or Pride?

Disobedience is painful. Believe me I know it caused incredible pain to all of us - but it is only fatal if it produces an outcome that cannot be redeemed. Jesus, The Older Brother - the Lamb of God - was always our way out. Elohim always included protection and redemption in the plan. The potential fatal problem with disobedience is when one locks oneself in a state of pride while restoration is made available.

Redemption provides a way out of paranoia into metanoia:[75] the alignment of our thoughts with our originators thoughts. Redemption gives us the perfect pitch to tune ourselves to. If the goal is to create an identity outside of God's blessing for us - which Eve and I did - we may run into a pride problem. Restoration is impossible where pride prevails.

Disobedience can teach us that our thinking was wrong. It can teach us to understand the devastating effects of our distorted mindset. In that case disobedience followed by a mind-shift, a change of thinking, has helped us mature into our true identity, producing lasting wisdom in the process.

Satan's purpose was to propose an alternate identity to Eve and I. Then the plan was to lock us into a state of wrong thinking with pride. Satan fears the humble that accept redemption by admitting their illogical, out-of-tune thought patterns. Disobedience can be dealt with; pride is difficult. You can't keep on singing out-of-tune in opposition to Heaven's symphony while sticking your fingers in your ears! Metanoia is an essential value in God's Kingdom.

The Tree of Knowledge of Good and Evil

God warned me: "Don't eat the fruit of the tree or you will die." [76] God didn't trick us, nor did He tempt us. God was determined to walk with us through to maturity as perfect parents do. Testing leads to maturity. James says, *“Consider it pure joy, my brothers and sisters, whenever you face trials of many kinds, because you know that the testing of your faith produces perseverance. Let perseverance finish its work so that you may be mature and complete, not lacking anything.*[77]

Satan tempted us, and he appealed to our immaturity proposing a shortcut into identity thereby short-circuiting our relationship with Abba, Amma and Older Brother. He played to what was already brewing in us. He deceived us into establishing for ourselves a counterfeit identity. Genesis 3 verses 1 to 5[78] highlights how Satan played to Eve’s desires to mature in her identity independently. All of the offerings of the forbidden tree appealed to our developing sense of identity. The tree offered a sense of freedom, power, independence and significance.

Satan added to our thought process another layer of temptation that caused us to go over the edge, so to speak. *"God knows that in the day you eat from it your eyes will be opened, and you will be like God.”* [79] In other words, he suggested that God was hiding something from us because he didn’t want us to achieve our full potential. This thinking is the big deception. It suggests two things: First, that Abba,

Amma and Older Brother are not what and who they say they are. Secondly that we are not who and what we could be. It caused doubt and confusion and, therefore, it led us to believe that we could create our identities to be like them without mirroring them!

Eve and I knew we needed to mature into our full identity. We needed to align and clarify our thinking - we needed to make up our mind according to God's thoughts about us. We were too eager to listen to the Serpent. Eve was first to agree with the lies and I followed suit. It's not the exercise of the will that is a problem; it is the exercise of will apart from God and one another that causes problems.

I desired revelation, provision, wisdom, beauty and recognition. The tree seemed to offer these things. They are natural desires of human nature – the problem is where and how we try to obtain these things. Believe me, God wants us to have them; He created us to enjoy them in Him and from Him, not apart from Him.

Human nature seeks significance. Significance is the byproduct of identity. In God, significance is understood with humility and a sense of honor; obtained selfishly significance is expressed with arrogance and pride. Pride locks us up in a state of paranoia. God resists the proud. Significance acquired apart from God produces shame! Shame is the curse of identity. When it is received from God, it produces honor. Identity without God is an illusion that leaves our hearts void of love and minds filled with lies. That single decision cut us off from our life-spring and light-source: God.

We left the world in a terrible state. We lost our Rulership over creation. Darkness took over because we cut ourselves off from the only source of light, creating a veil of separation. We can't see who we are anymore! We have become paranoid.

We've created an environment where our souls have been corrupted and every person seeks to establish their identity above the other - selfishness is rampant. We're out of tune. We've forgotten our songs. We are dissonant. Our collective voices have become a cacophony in the universe. It's easy to see how.

If you can't see who and what you are, you will seek to establish it by yourself - through your personal efforts. I see it in you. You work hard to acquire signs that give you an edge over those you want to impress. You buy the latest car for no other reason than to astound your friends, family and neighbors. You use money for self-exaltation; you acquire the most recent fashion in everything so you might have your fifteen minutes of glory. You use Facebook to promote yourself above others. You are never satisfied, always acquiring more and always robbing others of their glory: all this in worship of self-made identity. But it leaves you empty, doesn't it? You are paranoid. What a mess!

God's Master Plan

Our Divine Family factored disobedience into our maturing process within their Master Plan for Eternity. Abba, Amma and Older Brother want us with them in Heavenly places as Sons and Rulers forever, and the maturing process included learning to tune our hearts, minds and affections to Heaven's perfect pitch. They chose to teach us maturity within the Cosmos where time and space are limited. They determined to enable this process to take place outside of Eternity and Heaven where the consequences of our immaturity would have been eternally fatal. So they placed us within a limited place - the Cosmos - where they could redeem the misfortunes of our learning. (Time and space are a parenthesis in our eternal existence.)

The Cosmos is not just ours to rule over; it is our place of testing and maturing. It is a place of learning to align our souls to The Logos of our lives. We will enjoy Rulership forever once we have learned that God's thoughts are higher than our thoughts.

Eve and I chose to learn through disobedience and that caused all the evil and pain in the Cosmos. But because of Christ (Older Brother revealed in the Cosmos in Flesh and Blood) our disobedience is redeemable - indeed it has been redeemed. Pride or humility will determine the outcome.

Grace and forgiveness are antidotes for our selfish and paranoid ambitions.

Our fall and redemption teach us that our true identity is blessed in Christ and revealed to us in Him who reconciles us to our Heavenly Parents, not apart from Them. *"The fear of the LORD is the beginning of wisdom, And the knowledge of the Holy One is understanding."* [80] The outcome is Eternal!

Sin and Law – An Introduction

Sin is hideous. It is incredibly destructive. It's a horrible thing for parents to be estranged from their children. Even more so for creation to walk away from its Creator – for God's children to divorce themselves from their Heavenly Father. It has produced all the evil in the world. It has robbed us of our blessed identities. Sin and the subsequent behaviors of sin teach us that without a system of law to bring some form of order to a fallen world, society would be in deeper chaos than it is, no thanks to Eve and I. Law has brought some sanity into an otherwise uncivilized people. It also introduced religiosity. But, what sin and law teach us is that we desperately need God. They show us that we need to reconnect somehow with God to rediscover who we are. I was immature and subsequently foolish in my quest to assert my identity and I stepped out of Heaven's blessing, but they never changed their plan - their thoughts about and for us remain eternally the same!

Do you know what we learned through all this? Abba, Amma and Older Brother *do* love us unconditionally! And we can truly make wise decisions by accepting their offer of reconciliation and resurrection life in Jesus. As a result, we enter into an Eternal place of identity and destiny!

Chapter Six

I, Adam

Lecture No 6: I Am Deceived

"In the view of such harmony in the Cosmos
which I, with my limited human mind,
am able to recognize,
there are yet people who says there is no God."

Albert Einstein

Well... you are back. Come on in. Join us for the next lecture. It's great to see you.

So far we've talked about why Elohim created us, and we've delved into our unique design. We've also discussed the fact that they created us as free moral agents. From there we moved into understanding the thinking that led Eve and I to disobey God's commandment. We misaligned our thoughts from God's thoughts.

In this lecture, and in the ones to follow, I want to unpack the consequences of my disobedience. Consequences you face every day because of me. It will take a few lectures. I aim to help you understand the behaviors of fractured humanity and hopefully give you greater awareness of your troubles. There is hope - that's the good news! Jesus, who undid everything I did wrong, provides us with the vision to recapture everything I lost. I plunged us into the darkness of the abyss. He brings us back to the surface, into the light. Remember, Christ protected your innocence in Himself - He is the guardian of Truth. Are you ready? Let's do this!

When The Created Realm Overrules The Heavenly

To give in to the temptation, Eve and I had already taken our eyes off of the heavenly realm and our "I Am" in

Christ. We had made the earthly realm our primary focus and reference. In other words, we had turned "Rulership" into our main focus ahead of "Sonship." When "Rulership" overrules "Sonship" then the created realm overrides the heavenly. We slowly lost our focus, steadily losing sight, like cataracts gradually impairing our eyes. We stopped referencing our being (our "I Am") on Older Brother.

When we source our imaginations from the created realm, we easily give in to temptation.

Notice the form Satan took on when he approached Eve: he took on the appearance of a serpent. The serpent was one of the beasts of the field: God's creation. Eve and I were supposed to rule the serpent, not position ourselves face-to-face with him. When I named the animals in the first place, I found none to be like me, none I could relate to face-to-face, particularly not the serpent. We had an incredible relationship with Abba, Amma and Older Brother. In taking our eyes away from them, we began to feel the need to feed our need for affection from within the created realm rather than from Heaven. If God is not the soul's primary source of affections, the soul will turn its desires toward created things. If "Heaven" is not our first focus then "Creation" will fill the void. If Older Brother is not the reference of my "being" (my "I Am") then I, Adam the fallen (the Adamic), will become the reference. And I'm not a great example, believe me! That's idolatry. That's Paganism. That's Humanism.

We were moving toward our disassociation from God even before the serpent tempted us. The reflections seduced us instead of the reality. Satan saw the "crack" and exploited it. He drove a wedge in the gap by distorting our view of reality with his lies. He is good at that. The devil simply sped up a process that was already in motion. Remember the thinking process Eve and I entertained in the previous lecture?

Lies

The devil had been in conflict with God for a long time, and he had developed a means to oppose God: lies - the distortion of God's thoughts and words. Talking about the devil, Jesus says that, *"Whenever he speaks a lie, he speaks from his own nature, for he is a liar and the father of lies."*[81]

Lies deflect from the reality and establish distorted premises to our thought patterns by twisting our view of God's thoughts. Everything God creates is the outcome of his spoken thoughts (The Logos). God reveals His perfect plans to us. Creation becomes twisted and warped by lies. It's a perversion of Truth. Lies deform the goodness and perfection of the created realm as initially formed by God's Word. Lies are an attempt to deconstruct and reconstruct the creation into a twisted evil form reflecting the heart of the Liar. The Liar can't change the Truth, but he can twist our perception of it, even to the point of veiling from us its source.

Obedience, in the context of our relationship with Elohim, is therefore carrying out Their commandments. Commandments are a request to act upon their thoughts and plans. When Elohim speaks, Their words become creation. When they delegate the Logos, they share it with us in the form of a commandment. God's commandments carry as much life and creativity as His Words did when He created the Cosmos in the Genesis narrative.

Disobedience can be as simple as not carrying out a commandment because the original thought has been distorted. Obeying a lie is disobedience. Furthermore, lies fuel conflicts by introducing distrust into a relationship. Lies carry the sting of divorce (disassociation).

The devil understood this process because he had experienced it first hand. He once was Lucifer, one of God's top archangels; He divorced himself from God. All Satan needed to do was introduce a lie into our immature thought patterns, distorting the nature of our relationship with God to prime the process of separation, and that is what he did. The outcome of this process was not just paranoia, but perversion. It produced a deviant view of ourselves (who "I Am") as a corrupt understanding of God's thoughts.

We Disobeyed

Notice how subtle the lie was? Eve knew what God had said: an open defiance to that Word would have been too obvious to her. Satan was cunning. He only added a subtext to God's Word. "God said what he said because he does not want you to be everything you can be!" Reading subtexts into God's Word is dangerous. You must also be careful not to rely solely on physical evidence (the created realm) to explain things. It's like pointing at the mirror and declaring that the mirror is the substance. When you shatter the mirror you realize the substance is not in the mirror - the substance is what stands in front of the mirror. The mirror reduces what is real into a flat, emotionless and limited representation. Relying on physical facts is to be earthly focused and misses the fact that God speaks from Heaven which is the source of reality - Physical evidence alone cannot explain Heaven. God's Word needs to be understood from His perspective. The serpent gave a materialistic and physical interpretation to God's Word when he said, "You surely will not die!" From an "earthly" perspective that may have been true, but from a "heavenly" perspective our death would be immediate! We had shifted our focus away from the source, concentrating our attention on creation, the reflection. It was easy for Satan to veil Truth with his lies!

Slowly Eve and I began moving our being in agreement with God (our focus on Heaven) to being in accord with the serpent (a focus on Earth). In doing so, we positioned ourselves as slaves to the serpent. Paul puts it this way: *"Do you not know that when you present yourselves to someone as slaves for obedience, you are slaves of the one whom you obey...?"* [82] Satan had offered us a freedom proposition, but instead we got slavery. Thus, Eve and I agreed with the serpent, aligned our thoughts with lies and disobeyed God.

The Exchange

Immediately a screen between Heaven and Earth was created. Satan's lies became so thick that he completely veiled our understanding from Truth. Instead of seeing and understanding the World through spiritual knowledge, we became solely reliant on the created realm to know, think and feel. In other words, we only trust what we see and experience in the physical World, and since we cannot see the spiritual truths of Heaven anymore, we deny its reality. God became a myth. We started to worship creation. And we lost sight of our true identities.

The Apostle Paul makes the exact assessment of our fall in Romans chapter one:

"For since the creation of the world His invisible attributes, His eternal power and divine nature, have been clearly seen, being understood through what has been made, so that they are without excuse. For even though they knew God, they did not honor Him as God or give thanks, but they became futile in their speculations, and their foolish heart was darkened. Professing to be wise, they became fools, and exchanged the glory of the incorruptible God for an image in the form of corruptible man and of birds and four-footed animals and crawling creatures. Therefore God gave them over in the lusts of their hearts to impurity, so that their bodies would be dishonored among them. For they exchanged the truth of God for a lie, and worshiped and served the creature rather than the Creator, who is blessed forever. Amen."[83]

They exchanged the truth of God for a lie! Lies and darkness became our reality.

Lies have influenced our thought process instead of wisdom from above[84] - God's thoughts. As a result, we must rely on empirical data, logic, the physically visible, audible and tangible to guide us. The physical realm becomes the only reality; creation becomes god; idolatry becomes religion. We are in the dark: *"they exchanged the truth of God for a lie, and worshiped and served the creature rather than the Creator!"*

The greatest calamity in this is that we have lost sight of our blessed identities - our "I Am" realities in Christ. Our identities are hidden in Christ, but we've lost access to Him. We can't hear what they have to say about us from the Book-of-Life! We don't know who we are. We're out of tune and have lost our songs. The physical realm and myself (Adam) have become your only points of reference. Everything your forefathers became through time is what you are now. All the words spoken to and about you and your ancestors before you, are incarnate in you! You are living a lie!

Psalms 116 says, *"I said in my alarm, 'All men are liars.' "* [85] This is not because we speak lies, it is because we live a lie.

In a previous lecture, I mentioned how it was important for Jesus to restore to us our free-moral-agency. It was equally important that He restore our access to truth: to a restoration of our eyesight, a revelation of our original innocence. Jesus heals the blinded eyes and restores hearing to the deaf! We desperately need to listen and align our thoughts with God's heart and mind - His Logos about us and for us. We require a tearing away of the veil. Without that access, we remain in the dark and we live and know only lies.[86]

Heaven is the Kingdom of God. Heaven's reality is Truth. Lies keep us out of the reality of Heaven.[87] When Eve and I believed the serpent's lie, we cut ourselves off from Heaven.

From the moment of birth, the World teaches you lies reinforced by the fact that the only access to information is the physical body and the Adamic reference. Everything you think is true is a lie, or at least only partly true because you do not see the picture from its original place. We cannot see all the truth until we have Heaven's perspective – the spiritual perspective. "Creation" has become our sole filter for understanding our reality, but that is only one part of reality: a darkened and distorted reflection.

Nakedness, Darkness and Death

The Genesis narrative says, *"that the eyes of both of them were opened, and they knew that they were naked; and they sewed fig leaves together and made themselves loin coverings."* [88] Fig leaves are a poor substitute for God's Glory. I find the wording quite interesting: *"the eyes of both of them were opened"* really means that we lost sight of our spiritual makeup. At that moment, we were veiled to the reality of our spiritual genesis. Consequently, we could only "see" the new twisted form of the physical realm. We had lost our glorious clothing, and so we saw the physical body the way it was without the Glory and twisted by Satan's lies: naked and unworthy. We were ashamed of what we saw; it was so miserable, unattractive and degraded compared to the Glory we knew. Shame entered our hearts!

It's as if my spirit hid itself. As a result, I lost total connection with the Spiritual Realm. Our focus and awareness were solely in the created realm, and my spiritual sensitivity was dead. I lost communion with God and all my spiritual senses. That's spiritual death. The spirit's flame was snuffed out. Job puts it this way: *"Indeed, the light of the wicked goes out, And the flame of his fire gives no light. The light in his tent is darkened, And his lamp goes out above him."* [89] The tent in this passage refers to the physical bodies. The "light" is the spirit. Eve's and my flames went out above us – the light darkened in the tents of our physical bodies. We fell from glory as our spirits' lights went out. We had descended into spiritual darkness: spiritual deception!

The Apostle Paul tells us in his writings that, *"All have sinned and fall short of the glory of God."* [90] Indeed, we have fallen from the place of Glory – we have lost the glorious spiritual clothing.

Time

That wasn't our only problem! Our disobedience took us from a "now logic" (living in the eternal realities of Heaven reflected into the Cosmos in each moment) to "time logic." Time and space do not limit the now logic. The clock defines the “time logic.” Just as we changed our source of understanding from the supernatural to the natural, we also changed our understanding of “continuum.” From living in the "I AM” in the present eternal tense, we turned to "I WILL BE," pursuing something tomorrow as a result of our efforts and history. The Yesterday-Today-Tomorrow concept mixed with fear and the understanding of our limitations in a limited environment produced stress, anxiety and pain we weren’t created for. I, Adam, was formed on the sixth day to live in the NOW of the seventh day - The Sabbath - in the Presence of Abba, Amma and Older Brother. We had unlimited access to unlimited resources, and we rested in that. It was all ours in the NOW of every moment and the I AM of our identity in Christ. We knew no anxiety, no fear of tomorrow, no shame of failure... we lived in the eternity on Earth as it is in Heaven. One of the biggest concerns we faced after our disobedience was the inevitability of death; we knew, instinctively that it was just a matter of time!

Intellectual Belief

I observe you and often shake my head in disbelief at the belief systems you have developed as a result of living in the dark, but I know I only have myself to blame.

Darwinism, atheism, humanism and religion are the prominent outcomes of the mindset that worships Creation rather than the Creator. If there is no Heavenly reality, then it all makes sense to explain the Cosmos, the universe and nature this way. The Laws of Physics cannot be violated; they are undeniable. They are the beginning and end of all things! Biology dictates to us how the body works and how it can or cannot heal itself! If it is logical, empirical, proven by evidence, then it is believable, but if it is not then it must be refuted or explained away.

Cut off from Heaven we have only two choices. To become intellectually focused on materialism and the rational or to become like animals relying on carnal instincts (or a blend of both). Two types of "Man" have developed: "Intellectual Man" and the "Sensual Man" - both are a version of the carnal. Both find their reference in my fallen Adamic nature.

The problem is that this is the default mindset "intellectual man" uses to understand the Bible. Faith based on intellectual understanding is no faith at all. Faith placed in the things you can understand and explain within the natural realm is a form of science; it is a rational process. It is belief, but not faith. *"Faith is evidence of things unseen."* [91] Faith is the gift you need to reconnect with the hidden reality of Heaven.

Intellectual belief is often theoretical in nature. Theories are born out of lack of encounters with Truth. When one's "experiences" of life have remained limited and tarnished by fear, lies and shame, you can understand how that person's theories about life cannot reflect Heaven's reality. This type of belief system never ventures outside of what can be seen, heard and understood in the physical, natural and material realm. It's sad. And I know it's all my fault.

Believing Lies

The default tendency of the soul depleted of its only source of Truth is to believe lies. The Bible says, *"The god of this world has blinded the minds of the unbelieving so that they might not see the light of the gospel of the glory of Christ."* [92]

The result is that you believe every negative and critical word pronounced against you. You become the incarnation of lies. You store up mountains of toxic beliefs about yourself, God and others. You have developed theologies that repeatedly remind you that you are evil, sinners, compounding guilt and condemnation. You focus on sin and sinfulness rather than love and your sinless identity in Christ. Unforgiveness, hurts, anger and all sorts of ugliness fill your hearts because you have believed the lies. These toxic words are lies that curse your identity with shame.

The outcome is a world of evil: *"Then the LORD saw that the wickedness of man was great on the earth, and that every intent of the thoughts of his heart was only evil continually."* [93] That doesn't mean Man is evil; it means that the behaviors of a broken soul are wicked! Unrighteousness is living outside of God's original Logos!

If parents repeat to a child that he is lazy, then he will become lazy. If the child is regularly put down with negative, demeaning words, he will believe them. The child develops an inner-world of ugliness that shows fruit in its outer-world. Many parents see the fruit as the vindication of what they have been saying all along: "See, you are lazy!" These constant negative words, associated with the emotional pain they represent, develop an inner world of conflict, anger and hurt. This inner world becomes the child's reality, his identity, and the child grows believing there's nothing much they can do to change. Instead of living free out of a blessed self, they live enslaved to lies out of a cursed identity of shame. They become the incarnation of lies.

The reality is that this inner world will always evidence itself in the outer world: it is the world you create from what is in your soul: truth or lie. All the evil in the world today originated in the soul of fallen Man whose minds have been invaded by lies.

Chapter Seven

I, Adam

Lecture No 7: I Am Afraid

"Only when we are no longer afraid do we begin to live."

Dorothy Thompson

We've covered a lot of ground and before we move on I want to review some of the big ideas we've discussed in these lectures. There are ten big ideas we've covered in six lectures that I would like to highlight:

1. God created us for Sonship and Rulership;

2. God designed us to relate to both the created and uncreated realms;

3. The physical mirrors the spiritual. Our physical bodies reflect our spiritual personas. The spiritual is the substance; the physical is a mere reflection of the spiritual.

4. God is the originator and architect of our identities. Abba and Amma are the progenitors of our spiritual personas. We are the expression of the Trinity's love. Older Brother carried and protected us in Himself; I, Adam bore your DNA in myself; I am the progenitor of your physical bodies.

5. Our soul is designed to process information and act in such a way that the will and way of Heaven become the reality on Earth.

6. We are Holy beings because God uniquely designed us among all creation, set us apart for a unique purpose, and we remained untainted by evil in Christ. God created us entirely free.

7. We are free moral agents: we can act freely upon our wills in an environment of unconditional love, uncontaminated truth and God-blessed identities;

8. Maturity comes through the exercise of our will in obedience or disobedience to our Creators. Eve and I chose disobedience.

9. Love isn't forced upon us. Forced love is no love at all.

10. My disobedience "disconnected" us from the spiritual man in Heavenly places, created a veil between Heaven and Earth, plunging us into a world of deception cut off from God. It blinded us from seeing our true selves in Older Brother, tainting our vision of who we are, God, and the Cosmos around us.

In this lecture, I will unpack another consequence of our disobedience: fear!

Fear

The Genesis story goes like this:

"They heard the sound of the LORD God walking in the garden in the cool of the day, and the man and his wife hid themselves from the presence of the LORD God among the trees of the garden. Then the LORD God called to the man, and said to him, 'Where are you?' He said, 'I heard the

sound of You in the garden, and I was afraid because I was naked; so I hid myself.' " [94]

When we disobeyed God, fear possessed us. It terrorized us. Up until that moment, all Eve and I knew was the perfect Love of God. Perfect love ruled our emotions. Fear could not control us. Although we recognized it, fear was an unfelt emotion. Imagine the shock. For the first time we felt something incredibly distressing deep in our inner being: fear - more like terror. It was an overwhelming, uncontrollable sensation that we were not equipped to handle. It submerged us like a tidal wave! For the first time in our history fear entered the fabric of our beings and gave way to evil. Our dreams turned into a nightmare; the songs of our lives into disheartened ballads.

The soul that is separated from perfect communion with God loses the shield of perfect love that protects it from fear. David writes in Psalm 3: *"But You, O LORD, are a shield about me, My glory, and the One who lifts my head. ...I will not be afraid of ten thousands of people who have set themselves against me round about."* [95]

Fear is deadly. We can't cope with it. The antidote to fear is the presence of God where we dwell in unconditional love and remain in sight of truth. Fear does not abide in the light. But now, we've cut ourselves off from Heaven and our source of light. We dread the dark because it's fear's playground.

Lies are the building blocks of a dysfunctional world; fear is the mortar. Together lies and fear build walls and strongholds behind which we retrench ourselves in defense of our man-made identities and kingdoms. Fear fuels pride. Pride locks the door of redemption into maturity.

The Battle

It started with a lie. Remember, lies are a distortion of the reflection, but the original Word remains unchanged in God.

God said, *"You shall not eat from it* (the fruit of the tree of knowledge of good and evil) or touch it, *"or you will die."* [96] I believed God, but I was naive in my thoughts. I had a choice. Remember the thought process and questions I struggled with in my lecture about immaturity? Obedience required my total trust in God. A battle raged in my immature mind. I assumed that obeying God's commandments meant that Eve and I would miss out on knowledge. We lusted after knowledge. But we also feared the consequences of disobedience: death. Then came the lie. The Liar couldn't change the truth - the original thoughts and intent of God are immutable. So he twisted God's instructions to me. He lied! "You won't die, besides if you do not eat you will never reach your full potential. You will become insignificant. And, by the way, God doesn't want you to reach that potential. He is hiding something from you. There's something you don't know about God that He doesn't want you to know."

The lies produced paranoia in our heart and minds. Eve and I feared insignificance more than death itself. Knowing everything, and how to discern good and evil would be a very handy thing to possess when you're supposed to remain at the top of your game. We feared not knowing because that meant insignificance. On the other hand, we also feared death as a consequence of disobedience. Fear exists in a perfect environment - outside the walls of our protective shield - but it never possessed us until we disobeyed. It was an emotion that allowed us to remain aware of our environment. We could use it to process things in order to act appropriately. God's shield of love protected us from its terrorizing power. Fear surrounded us, but did not control us. Perfect love banishes fear. God instructed us with Truth; They guided us with love. They encouraged us from a position of honor!

The battle of fear had started in my heart and mind a long time before fear possessed my soul and embittered my heart. Fear surrounded me and was crouching ready to pounce at me and envenom me with its vicious poison at any time. It was never a ruling emotion. Peace ruled my heart until I removed myself from Elohim's shield, allowing it to sting me.

Paranoia is a battle of fears. Two armies were engaged in the conflict: "fear of punishment" on one hand, versus "fear of insignificance" on the other. The battleground: my mind! The healthy thing would have been to respect the consequences of disobedience because God had highlighted that issue. But instead, I placed more weight on the fear of insignificance because I lusted after knowledge. Knowledge is power.

There is healthy fear (respect) and unhealthy fear (terror). Healthy fear is a protection. Terror produces panic and paralysis. It also places us in a constant state of anxiety. A fearful emotion that approaches us while we remain in perfect love and peace is a warning. We ignored the signs because we were too eager to position ourselves in a place of self-made significance. The fear of insignificance outweighed a healthy respect of the consequence. A fearful emotion that possesses and terrorizes you leads to uncontrollable and unthinkable behaviors. There is a difference between respect of fear, with its varying shades of warnings, and, the infection of fear with all our emotions being overtaken by its poison. Fear is a good servant, but a terrible master. You can't partner with the serpent without getting stung.

We feared insignificance most. This fear outweighed everything else. We feared it more than death. Therefore, we chose to deal with it outside of God's will and protective love.

We feared insignificance and we got what we feared. Job says, *"What I fear comes upon me, And what I dread befalls me."* [97] Take this as a warning: Do not focus on the things you fear most. Focus on God! Remain under Their (Abba, Amma and Older Brother's) protective shield, even if it means you feel insignificant. Whatever you fear and try to resolve or avoid outside of God's Perfect Love and outside the Logos will come upon you because you're unprotected - naked. If you fear slavery and seek freedom outside of The Logos, you will find yourself a slave to somebody or something. The Logos, which is found in the presence of God where perfect love abides, is a protection from fear even when fear encompasses you. Love is God's glorious protective clothing.

A free moral agent bathed in The Logos can process fear with a clear mind. In my immaturity, I had already moved away from focusing on Heaven. I was placing too much weight on my significance as ruler. I was losing my ability to decide between which emotion to respect and which one to reject. To decide (decision) is the capacity to separate, to cut away, to make incisions: to recognize or refuse. As long as I knew how to discern fear and how to separate and dismiss, I could make healthy choices and act upon my will according to God's will. This discernment was possible when I had their thoughts. Eve and I felt we could gain that ability by accessing knowledge of good and evil. We thought we could kill two birds with one stone: gain knowledge (with significance as the prize) and avoid death. We disobeyed. Immediately we were cut off from God, their presence and their perfect love. Fear flooded our souls like a tsunami. Fear terrorized us. Our song became a bitter complaint. Fear poisoned the waters that flowed from our wells.

Slavery to Death

Immediately we feared God in a negative way. We regarded Him as our Judge, instead of Father. Since my fall, religion has perpetuated this idea throughout the ages. The healthy fear of death turned into a terror that possessed us. The punishment for our disobedience petrified us: *"fear involves punishment, and the one who fears is not perfected in love."*[98]

This warped view of God is the direct outcome of Satan's suggestion that God was hiding something about His nature to us. We put two and two together: *"God doesn't want us to discover the Tree of Knowledge of Good and Evil. He doesn't want us be Judge over Creation because He is Judge."* What a Lie! Elohim created us for Sonship and Rulership, not to judge us. Abba doesn't judge us.[99] Abba delegated all judgment to Older Brother, and he has decided to judge nobody.[100] Our names have always been in the Book. At the end of the day, it will always be our choice as to whether or not we show up for the roll call. Believe me, life in the Adamic reference I engendered is no life at all. There's a better one for you: Resurrection Life in Christ. Choose wisely!

Evil

Then came darkness. I was completely cut off from reality, the origin and genesis of my being. Now, I can't see. My only reference is creation invaded by lies. All I see is a grotesquely deformed reflection. Heaven is invisible. The Liar has invaded our world.

Evil is the distorted effects of the lie that mirrors the nature of the Liar. He is twisted. He bends God's good creation out of shape. Have you ever seen a two-headed snake? You already fear "normal" snakes because of our encounter in the garden (that memory is in your genes); try a double-headed one! Lies have distorted the physical realm. You have lost the knowledge of who you are and see yourself as a perversion of your perfect design. Creation is in captivity. You see the outworking of all these lies in their truest form: evil. It is revealed in our thought patterns, behaviors, in the broken, the twisted, the perversions, from our beliefs and actions to our broken families and suffering bodies. Can you see the outworking of lies all around you?

Cancer is a cell that has believed a lie and shows the twisted nature of the Liar.

We fear evil. Evil lurks in the dark waiting to pounce and torment its unsuspecting prey. But evil is only a twisted form of God's perfect original design and Word. Evil has no substance. The Liar can't change the original perfect Logos. The Logos has never lost its holiness. The You in Christ was always protected in Him.

There is no battle between good and evil; there is Truth and a distorted version of it reflected into the Cosmos. Eve and I gave our authority to the serpent's lie granting it power over us. It's all about how many layers of lies we've allowed to build up between us and Truth.

The Psalmist declared: *"Even though I walk through the valley of the shadow of death, I fear no evil, for You are with me; Your rod and Your staff, they comfort me."* [101] He feared no evil because he knew he was dealing with a shadow in the darkness. He remained aware that he was protected and shielded in Yahweh's perfect love.

Darkness

We've lost sight of everything. We walk in the shadow, but we have no light to direct our paths. Our view of God is a gross mischaracterization of His true nature. Our representation of humanity is warped and demeaning. We've lost the vision of our true identity. Our theories about the reality of Creation are utterly misleading. Our philosophies are misconstruing. That's not truth. It is not reality. It's all a deformed and twisted reflection of dimmed light through a dark prism of unthinkable lies. It's like looking in a darkened and deformed mirror.

But Elohim never lost sight of us. They are determined to accompany us through to maturity. And they always seem to get what they want. Light has visited us and will prevail. Older Brother has kept the Book, the symphony of Heaven, the blueprints of our lives in Himself. He died to give you resurrection life, to bring you into the light. Abba awaits at the door for your return with a cloak to cover your shame and a ring to remind you of your family ties. The blood that was poured out at the altar of the Lamb's Sacrifice, at the cross of Jesus' Calvary, stays before Them in Heaven's Temple as a proof of your family belonging. And Amma, well she keeps gently calling your name, proclaiming truth, patiently drawing you to a place where you'll finally come to your senses. God is passionately devoted to Mankind.

Fear of Light

The narrative goes like this: *". . . the man and his wife hid themselves from the presence of the LORD God among the trees of the garden."* [102] We ran from God's presence! Further on I explain to God why: *"I heard the sound of You in the garden, and I was afraid because I was naked!"* [103] The author of Hebrews says that humankind became held in slavery by their fear of death. [104] Perhaps the deepest fear you, Sons-of-Adam, brought into this world in my fallen likeness, have to deal with since my fall, is the fear of light.

Is it possible that the reason you fear death so much is because, beyond death, there is resurrection for all. Not resurrection through our efforts, but resurrection in Christ, the Son-of-God, our Older Brother. And, in His resurrection we come into the light. Nothing can hide in the light. It's not hell we fear most because we've created our own version of it. Is it our shame we fear because we know we are naked, and we fear exposure in the light?[105] Is it because we fear judgment that we fear resurrection? Or maybe we fear more than that - a deeper truth. Do we apprehend that our cloaks of glory await us, that Abba can't wait to clothe us again? Is it forgiveness that bothers us most because we think we don't deserve it? Or is it our power that scares us; that we can't handle it? We wear our shame like a beggar's coat, and we hide from Their presence. Time to stop beating yourself up Sons-of-God. Jesus has taken the beating for you!

The Curse

As I described in my first few lectures, the soul has three primary functions. It uses each function to process information received from its spiritual and physical surroundings. The result of this process activates the will. If the soul is pure and uncorrupted by lies, fear and shame, it can process the information in total freedom, and the outcome is the best possible decision one can make. That's what it means to be a free moral agent.

The direct impact of fear entering into the soul is the immediate corruption of Man's heart, mind and ability to relate to others. Fear distorts our emotions, intellect and our ability to relate. It impairs our hearts, minds and affections. In turn, it affects our decision-making process. The outcome is distorted because of our impaired will. The results are cursed and dysfunctional.

Genesis 3:14-19[106] describes the curse that followed our disobedience. Most interpretations of this passage lead you to believe that God placed a malediction on us. That is not totally the case. God merely stated the consequences of our actions. Our souls had been invaded by lies and fear; our hearts, minds and affections would create a cursed environment. God was saying that because we had disobeyed, and fear had entered our world, childbearing would become painful for our wives. And we wouldn't enjoy the bonds of intimacy and oneness we once knew as man and woman in the garden. Fear's offspring is pain. Because we have been cut off from God and the Heavenly Realm, we would turn to providing food for ourselves through painful toil. God did not simply curse us: He described the new world we had created for ourselves.

A soul corrupted by lies and fear breeds three main dysfunctions: shame disables the ability to relate; deceit challenges the intellect; anxiety impairs the emotions. All three combined, weaken the will and bear fruits of wickedness.

Summary

The table on the next page summarizes the three functions of the soul by bringing together concepts visited so far throughout my lectures. You will remember the initial version of this table. I have added a section that reflects the outcome of lies and fear invading our souls.

"Parts" of The Soul	**Functions of The Soul**	**Functional Soul in Relationship with God**	
		Divine Input: Logos	**Harmonious Output: "Ruling Values"**
Heart	Emotional	Unconditional **Love**	Peace
Mind	Rational	Uncontaminated **Truth**	Wisdom
Affections	Relational	God-Blessed **Identity**	Honor
The WILL as outcome of processing our thoughts, emotions and affections		My Will is in Harmony with God's Will = Free Will (Freedom)	A Prosperous Soul = Prosperous Lifestyle & Healthy Body

"Parts" of The Soul	**Functions of The Soul**	**Dysfunctional Soul**	
		Defective Input: Sin	**Crippled Output: Unrighteousness**
Heart	Emotional	Fear	Anxiety
Mind	Rational	Lies	Deceit
Affections	Relational	Curse	Shame
The WILL as outcome of processing our thoughts, emotions and affections		A Bound Will =>	Dysfunctional Lifestyle & Unhealthy Body

A broken soul is contaminated and corrupted as a result of breaking our ties with our Creator. Fear overthrows love, deception defeats truth, and shame curses our Identity. The result is a bound will leading to a dysfunctional lifestyle and unhealthy body as anxiety, deceit and selfishness cripple our souls. The "fruits" of this lifestyle are also evident: they are called the works of the flesh.

We are only truly free in an environment where unconditional love, uncontaminated truth and a God-blessed identity rule. In other words, when these elements are absent, our freedom to make healthy choices is hampered. The decision Eve and I made introduced an environment that robbed all humanity of its free moral agency. Humanity has become slaves to sin, fear and the devil; therefore, in that environment, our wills are bound, our decisions mistaken, our world dysfunctional.

Chapter Eight

I, Adam

Lecture No 8: I Am The Sinner

*"Most of us think of pride as self-centeredness,
conceit, boastfulness, arrogance, or haughtiness.
All of these are elements of the sin,
but the heart, or core, is still missing.
The central feature of pride is enmity
-enmity toward God
and enmity toward our fellowmen."*

Ezra Taft Benson

For thousands of years, religion has kept its zealots enslaved to fear by making "sin" the central issue. Thus giving "sin" license to keep humanity separated from Abba, Amma and Jesus. Any concept that keeps us enslaved to fear is a travesty of truth. Lies have perverted The Logos' reflection into our World and when fear partners with falsehood they produce shame. Shame robs us of our glorious original identities. It keeps us singing bitter complaints.

Religion has made sin the main issue and focus of its dogmas, practices and ordinances. That's wrong - it's evil. This practice has tyrannized believers and produced as much shame as every other evil in the world. Wars produce pain and shame. Slavery caused much torment and disgrace. Religion's offsprings are guilt and humiliation.

Don't get me wrong, there needs to be a term used to designate the fall from Glory - my disobedience - and I hope to put it in its right place in this series of lectures. But if the doctrine enslaves you to fear and produces shame then somewhere a lie has distorted the original intent and thoughts of Elohim. God wants you to understand what happened in the Garden of Eden for the purpose of freedom and adoption: that's the intent. If the doctrine enslaves you to guilt, condemnation and dread - all various forms of fear - it's because lies have distorted it mirroring the heart of the Liar.

Having said that, let's talk about sin!

A Dysfunctional World

Our soul creates our world: a dysfunctional soul will create a dysfunctional world. We've made that clear. Jesus explains this in Mark 7.

"Listen to Me, all of you, and understand: there is nothing outside the man which going into him can defile him; but the things which proceed out of the man are what defile the man. "If any man has ears to hear, let him hear." [107]

Jesus says that there is nothing that enters into your "inner man" from the physical world that can defile you, but it's what comes out of your inside world that will defile you. It's how you process the information that comes in, according to the state of your soul, that determines the outworking. When you express and act upon what is in your inner man, you create your world. You become what is in your soul based on the state of your inner man.

The disciples didn't get it, so they ask Jesus for an explanation, and He answers: *"That which proceeds out of the man, that is what defiles the man. For from within, out of the heart of men, proceed the evil thoughts, fornications, thefts, murders, adulteries, deeds of coveting and wickedness, as well as deceit, sensuality, envy, slander, pride and foolishness. All these evil things proceed from within and defile the man."* [108]

We have the potential within that becomes reality when we decide to act upon it. The outworking is inevitably evil because our hearts are filled with lies, fear and shame. It's the reality of people who have cut themselves off from God. We have no choice, but to act in agreement with the flesh.

Wickedness is the distortion of the Logos processed through deception, terror and dishonor. Satan only needed to prime the process. Since the original lie, we've spawned self-made deceptions, feeding our fears the steroids they need to grow into uncontrollable proportions. It's all cause and effect: the outcome of a defective soul.

A dysfunctional soul creates a dysfunctional world! The direct impact of fear entering into the soul is that it immediately corrupted the functioning of man's heart, mind, and ability to relate to others. Fear distorts the emotions, intellect and our sense of identity. It poisoned the soul. It rendered the decision-making process ineffective. The outcome is a distorted will. This process produces cursed results.

When the Spirit is "dead" the flesh prevails. There is no way to control our carnal ways outside of reconnecting ourselves with the Spirit. There are two reasons among others that I would like to highlight. The first reason is this: without "hearing" from Heaven the only source of awareness comes from the physical world: materialism, senses and instincts rule us. The second reason is that without perfect love in the heart, lies, fear and shame have become our inner man's motivation. The flesh has become the only functioning body feeding the soul; therefore it will always act "according to the flesh."

I see you're getting a bit edgy right now. You want to know the definition of sin I promised you. I like suspense!

"What is Sin?" What are your thoughts?

The typical definition revolves around immorality and behavior. But the problem is this: frequently the moral and behavioral standards change depending on the culture and environment in which one lives. There are further complications in the fact that often moral and behavioral ideals are unattainable. Every culture and religion throughout time has placed unreasonable and unattainable standards for its people to abide by. Yes, I know, I was the culprit, but what I'd like to suggest is that sin is not the breaking of those moral and behavioral standards you set for yourself in your cultural and religious environments. I understand that Moses' Ten Commandments are not ten suggestions, but breaking them is a legal issue that does not affect our relationship with God. The reasons I say this are because: (1) obeying the ten biggies doesn't fix the relationship with God in the first place, so why would breaking them damage the relationship? And (2) I have already broken the relationship with them, so it can't get worse can it? The codes are good and regulate life in a fallen environment. Every society needs them. But our right standing with God doesn't come through behavioral and moral policing.

Besides, we've established that behaviors are the outcome of lies and fear that inturn produce shame. Shame has robbed us of our identity. What you have come to believe about yourself is a long string of lies. Like a distorted double helix passed on from generation to generation or diminished copies of a poor quality original, each iteration slipping further from the original version. You can't be surprised at the state of this World. We created it. It's evil yes, but sin it is not.

So what is Sin? Can you answer this question without putting morality and behavior in the mix? Probably not! That's because religion has made morality and behavior the main issue. How can you expect holy perfection from inferior quality copies whose originator (me, Adam) had lost his initial flawlessness in the first place? The Adamic reference bears no resemblance to the glorious original: that's why Jesus came and walked among us. Jesus shows us what the original blueprint looks like, doing life in the midst of a fallen culture.

I give it to you that morality and behavioral changes occur once a person finds resurrection life and restoration in Christ - that's inevitable. But the opposite is true too: it is possible for the proud to change their behavior without there having been a change in heart and mind.

It's frustrating, isn't it, not to have a clear understanding of what sin is particularly since the issue of "salvation from sin" seems to reside at the core of the religious message? What if the central idea and point of Christianity is about the restoration of our Identities into the original blueprint held in Christ, The Logos? The distortion has never bothered Abba, Amma and Older Brother because they've kept the originals in their perfect, holy original condition. In other words, the behavior on Earth reflects evil and shame because of lies and fear. It hurts you on Earth, but it is not your reality in Christ. The thing that pains God the most is the pride that keeps us imprisoned in this lifestyle.

Let me give you some thoughts to consider:

God did not create us as Sons-of-God to be independent, self-focused individuals. God created us for community and connection. We are wired for interdependence with one another and dependence on Abba, Amma and Older Brother. They are our Creators. We depend on them for everything we need to rule over the works of Their hands. We exist In them as Sons. We are Sons-of-God existing first and foremost in God-The-Son before taking on this physical form. The spiritual endures way beyond the physical. We find and express our true identity from this reality, which means that the primary issue of Christianity, the heart of the matter, is and has always been about our identity and original design in Christ. Elohim has always wanted us as adopted sons! Adoption (mature Sons) has always been God's primary focus. He is at war with anything and anybody that robs us of that. He wants us to sing our song in the symphony of ages. Our voice in His composition matters. Your identity and destiny in Christ is the central issue.

Before eating the fruit of the Tree of Knowledge, Eve and I had no sense of independence and individualism. God created us in His Image. God is Trinity, and the three persons of the Trinity live in total submission to each other in interdependence. They created us to function that way: together and in them. Eve and I had no need for self-reliance; we had not experienced selfishness. We were at one with God and each other. Our identities are an extension of God's being and one another. And that is important. We cannot be mature Sons-of-God independently of them and each other.

When we ate the fruit of the Tree of Knowledge, we became self-conscious: individual-conscious. We became self-aware in a dimension that God had not intended for us: a dimension of separateness and selfishness.

To access the Tree of Knowledge of Good and Evil one must first believe the lie: "You will be like God!" When one conceives that possibility, the trust once placed in God is no longer relevant, nor necessary. Consequently, confidence is placed in self: the abilities, resourcefulness and experience of the individual take precedence over everything God and others have to offer. Selfishness prevails. What a lie. To think that Eve and I believed it is preposterous!

So are you ready for that definition? Here it comes:

Sin is Creation (as a free moral agent) saying to the Creator, "I do not need you." It is the Son rejecting the Father declaring, "You are nothing to me." I will be myself! I will make my identity by myself!

That's it! Simple!

Another way to look at it is this way: **Sin is the "killing off" of the divine Father figure resulting in the Son becoming an orphan.**

When Eve and I ate of that Tree of Knowledge of Good and Evil, we rejected God. It is as if we said to them, "We will be like You; therefore, we do not need You - we will create our identities"! That is deeply offensive and hurtful. I can imagine how they felt at that moment. I am ashamed of what I did. We established self over God, and we immediately saw that we were naked; we instantly became self-conscious!

The Greek word for "sin" means "to offend and to have no part." The moment that Eve and I decided that we would have no part with God because we thought we could gain significance apart from God, we hurt them deeply - we offended. That is Sin! Sin is not the behavior - it's the attitude that opened our world to lies and fear that in turn became the cause of all evil action.

The point of Christianity is not to police morality and behavior. Broken morals and corrupt behavior are the "normal" outworking of lies, fear and shame. You can't change the action without a restoration of relationship and return to the original blueprints of our lives. That's what Jesus died for. Of course that single act of redemption saves us from lies, fear and shame... and that is a process that takes time.

God does not rank sin. There is only one offense. Eve and I committed that offense. Everything else is the outworking of terror and deception. Divorce, estranged bitter relationships, sicknesses, disease, mental illnesses, murder, incest, hatred, drunkenness, addictions, wars, etc., are the outcome of my sin. Nobody else committed that offense, just Eve and I.

Many of you continue to reject Abba, Amma and Older Brother, of course, but that's because of the deception and fright I introduced into this world. I committed the offense! I am the sinner. I take responsibility. You, however, are an orphan because of me. And that is not a deliberate action on your part. You were born into an orphaned planet ruled by lies, fear and shame.

Did all this surprise God? Not a single moment. Obedience or disobedience: both roads lead to maturity. Perhaps the bigger problem, more pernicious than the contravening of moral standards and the breaking of the religious law, is pride. A haughty man will never understand how broken and distorted he is; he will never want to be restored because he is "great" in his own eyes. Will such a person show up for the roll call?

Chapter Nine

I, Adam

Lecture No 9: I Am On A Quest

*"Consciously or not, we are all on a quest for
answers, trying to learn the lessons of life.
We grapple with fear and guilt.
We search for meaning, love, and power.
We try to understand fear, loss, and time.
We seek to discover who we are
and how we can become truly happy."*

Elisabeth Kubler-Ross

The Empty Soul

I committed the only sin humankind ever perpetrated; the only one that matters! The rest, those things we label "sin," are the flow-on effect of that single act. As a result, my soul was cut-off from the essential Heaven-sourced elements needed to sustain our very existence: truth, love, and identity. I, Adam, became fearful instead of love-filled, materialistic-minded and deceived in the absence of truth, ashamed instead of living from my blessed self. I am a crippled orphan lamed by anxiety, deceit and selfishness!

The mind that is void of truth will tend to believe lies. That's obvious! What I experienced was that, in the absence of truth, I developed a new belief system sourced in the physical realm solely based on my experiences. Emotions accompanied every new experience. I used my emotions as a means to determine my reality. I walked like a blind man relying on touch and smell to assess my surroundings. I believed what my senses and logic told me. My experiences became my reality cemented into my belief system by my fearful emotions. In this state, the heart blinds us to all truth because it adds fear to lies cementing them into our belief system as an undeniable reality.

Lies have become the building blocks of our self-made edifices. Cemented together with the mortar of our fears to create impenetrable fortresses built to keep God and others out.

And so we, humankind - as one body, The Body-of-Adam - went on a quest for truth, love, and identity. We are orphans looking for our home, but seeking in the wrong places. We are musicians and singers with no instruments to play and no melody to sing: the dissonance of our songs echoing aimlessly through the empty valleys of creation. Prisoners of a senseless existence, we feel doomed to roam and wander throughout history, from past to present, on a crusade to find a clue that will make sense of it all.

The quest for truth is difficult because we tend not to see truth even when it's plain. We need healing from spiritual blindness! Over the years, we fill our heart with lies: lies about ourselves, people, God and everything. Because the heart is empty, we fill it. Nature abhors a vacuum; our souls must be saturated with something. We source truth solely from the created realm convinced that what we see, hear, touch, quantify and prove scientifically and rationally is the reality.

Not only is the heart emptied of truth, but it is also void of love. Truth and love work hand in hand as do lies and fear. Love without truth is a lie. Truth without love is hurtful.

However, truth and love without a healthy identity – a sense of significance and value – is meaningless. As a matter of fact, a cursed soul cannot assimilate truth and love.

It dwells in shame. It's a little bit like eating healthy food. If you have filled your body with toxins by drinking caffeine, soda, and alcohol and eating junk food, your digestive system becomes impaired. The unhealthy toxic lifestyle prohibits you from assimilating the healthy foods you may be eating. You need a detox. It is the same with your soul – a cursed identity cannot adequately absorb healthy uncontaminated truth and unconditional love.

A blessed identity gives us the freedom to relate. Unconditional love sets our hearts free. Uncontaminated truth empowers the mind to apply wisdom from above freely. The empty soul is deceptive and evil in all its ways. Genesis 6 says, *"Then the LORD saw that the wickedness of man was great in the earth, and that every intent of the thoughts of his heart was only evil continually."* [109]

The Primary Quest of Life

As a corporate people - "in Adam" -, we go through "life" with a need to fill our empty hearts with love, truth and identity. In our fallen state, this has become our primary quest. We seek to fill up our empty souls with the three essential elements of Life that are meant to be sourced from Heaven. Instead, we experience at best a flawed understanding of love and for most we experience rejection and hurt not knowing what love is and how to love. As far as truth is concerned, we are so easily deceived. Most people go through life with a broken and cursed identity. All this is the direct result of my sin. I cut us off from Heaven. I "killed" the spiritual man. I caused us to become as orphans crippled by anxiety, deceit and selfishness!

Our Creators designed our hearts to be connected to them and to respond to them because they are the only source of pure unconditional love, uncontaminated truth, and blessed identity. But when we are cut off from them, we seek others to fulfill our needs and it doesn't work; if it works at first, it seems to fall apart after a while.

Christ (The Last Adam) and I (Adam, the first, before the Fall) both lived in connection to God by our spirits: our quest was not about seeking love, truth and identity. A person enjoying wholeness (only available in Christ) doesn't need to find love, truth and identity. Such a person lives in and from the reality of a blessed Identity, with a heart filled with unconditional love and a mind motivated by uncontaminated truth. Their quest is simply to enjoy Sonship and to rule over the works of God's hands - each One according to their God-Given abilities! They have found healing from the orphan spirit. The quest of fallen man is a distraction from living our true purpose. Don't misunderstand me though: you need full restoration and wholeness of your soul first to live out your purpose, but recovery isn't the end game. Destiny is its purpose.

Everything we do in our orphaned state is driven by this quest for love, truth and identity. God wants your restoration so you can go beyond that pursuit. Instead of a healthy diet the orphan satisfies his needs with a twisted understanding of love and has built a belief system in response to the negative experiences of life. We've designed a worldview on how we ought to live our lives (career, finance, house, mortgage, car, materialism) based on lies while seeking the approval of society. We conform to this worldview, so we can fit in and be significant. All in this quest for love, truth and identity.[110] We say we need things that we don't, but we crave them to be approved and accepted. We build our lives on earthly treasures and materialism. We confuse status symbols for necessities because we need them emotionally to fit in, to be accepted and loved.

Until we find what we are looking for, our souls remain empty and thirsty. We can only satisfy what we thirst for in God, in His Kingdom, in His Spirit.[111] Jesus satisfies that intense desire: *"Let anyone who is thirsty come to me and drink. Whoever believes in me, as Scripture has said, rivers of living water will flow from within them."* [112]

When I say that Heaven is our source, it's not about drawing waters *from* the well to fill our buckets: it's about being in the spring and the wellspring flowing in and from you.

Our worst conduct is the outcome of this relentless pursuit. Paul puts it this way:

"Now the works of the flesh are obvious: sexual immorality, impurity, depravity, idolatry, sorcery, hostilities, strife, jealousy, outbursts of anger, selfish rivalries, dissensions, factions, envying, murder, drunkenness, carousing, and similar things." [113]

Think of it. How many of those "works of the flesh" aren't about twisted misconceived love or the outcome of love disappointed? We do terrible things in our quest to satisfy the needs of our empty souls. Sometimes we do good things as well, but not GOD things...

God's Way

God is Unconditional Love. God is Uncontaminated Truth. God is the source of everything you need. He provides. He is your wisdom. He is a well that will never run dry. He has created you significant and unique. But His ways are not your ways. You can't access what you crave and thirst outside of Him. And you can't do it your way. You can't use "materialistic" logic and fearful emotions to access the restoration of your soul.

Christ has an invitation for you to come into a restored relationship with Abba, Amma and Older Brother and into the resurrection of your Spirit. When you come to Christ, accepting the invitation to Redemption and Restoration, you find everything you need. I must stress at this point that this is not a transaction. It's not coming to God in Christ to fill your bucket. Restoration is reconnection. A re-union occurs with and in Them. That's the only way this can work.

It is in this union that the original blueprints of our lives is slowly poured back into us replacing the warped and faded copies with the original untainted version. It is there that your original song in Christ is made known to you replacing the old tunes of despair. You don't receive a new song; you become at one with the symphony, the creators and the artists.

Too often I see so many of you go about this the wrong way because you think that God is going to give you all the external things, the circumstantial improvements that you desire. Elohim doesn't want to fill your cup; they want to connect you to the spring so that your cup will overflow. You don't need improvements in your circumstances; you need to reconnect with the source of Life. God won't deal with things on the surface; He doesn't even fix the internal problems. It's better than that!

I've seen too much superficial self-improvement programs that leave people emptier at the end than when they started. And when God doesn't fulfill your cosmetic needs, you think there must be something wrong with you. Your old thinking hasn't changed. You think that you haven't done enough to be accepted by God. So you start performing, working on your weaknesses, and suppressing the ugliness of your temptations. You try to earn God's acceptance. That's wrong. Christ is the end of your quest. He is the healing of the orphan spirit.

God doesn't fulfill the needs of fallen human nature in a way that "feeds" the fallen man. That would be counter-productive. He just kills off the old man (Adam) and resurrects a new man (Christ) that strangely resembles me, Adam the first. This second Adam (Christ) is Son-of-God. He dealt with my sin. He is not an orphan and will not allow us to remain in the orphanage of the old Adamic nature. This New Adam is totally fulfilled in community with God, not apart from them and has no need to pursue the old quest. This Adam is completely satisfied in God's Unconditional Love and Uncontaminated Truth and demonstrates a genuine sense of blessed and mature Identity. He bears a new name! The pursuit of this new Adam is to introduce you to your Identity as Son-of-God and to pour into you the essence of who and what you've always been in Christ. The quest is over! You're in the symphony. You can sing your song. This second and last Adam has invited you to join Him in the reality of love, truth and blessed identity.

Chapter Ten

I, Adam

Lecture No 10: I Am The Body of Death

"No one wants to die. Even people who want to go to heaven don't want to die to get there. And yet death is the destination we all share. No one has ever escaped it. And that is as it should be, because Death is very likely the single best invention of Life.
It is Life's change agent.
It clears out the old to make way for the new."

Steve Jobs

To imbue the next few lectures with some intelligibility, I need to retrieve from the background of these lectures a theological idea in order to expand upon it. I have alluded to this thought right from the beginning without going into many details. You'll recognize the theme. It's time to develop. It won't take long, but it's a necessary clarification.

The Body of Adam

At creation, I, Adam, was "the firstborn of all creation." Our Creators consider every person born into this world after me as being "in me," "in Adam." Physically speaking, all the human race was in me, "in Adam," in my DNA - my loins - before anyone else was born. The significance of this needs to be appropriately discerned. When it comes to the Human Race in physical form, God sees nobody as individuals. He sees me, Adam, as one Body incorporating into myself all of humanity. Your legal stance before God is corporate - not personal. From a personal point of view, it all hinges on the body you belong to. You'll discover later in these lectures that there is a second body - a new creation – offered to Humanity.

The outcome of Eve's and my disobedience is that all the Human Race comes together as a fearful, materialistic-focused, shame-filled, sin-conscious, spiritually-dead body of people in me: The Body-of-Adam. And, I, Adam, am broken.

Every son and daughter is a copy of a copy referencing our "living" from the previous Adamic-like deteriorated generation. It just gets worse from copy to copy. Since I was cut off from Heaven, you have referenced and taken your sense of identity from the previous generation. The current form of "man" bears no resemblance to the original me. Lies after lie, from father to son, increased fear and evil has produced a body of people today that is far from God's original Logos spoken into creation at the emergence of our history. There has been a devolution of Mankind!

I will use my name "Adam" to refer to the corporate body. Anxiety, deceit and selfishness cripple the Body-of-Adam. The members of the Adamic Body pursue their quest in a dog-eat-dog environment. It's the survival of the fittest! You are all orphans belonging to an orphaned body.

I incorporated within my loins a stunning, brilliant and genius race of beings who today aren't able to live up to their potential because their souls have been corrupted, and their true identities hidden from them. The good news is that Christ has kept the blueprints of our innocence safe, but it will take a supernatural act to reconnect us to us to our true identities. Elohim has planned it all from before time.

Physically this race is God's creation and bears a resemblance to Him, but they've lost their glory - the Glory of God bestowed upon them at creation - and they are diminished in their faculties. Every individual born into this world - this created realm - from myself till the last baby - originate physically in my loins - you are all members of the Body-of-Adam. But my DNA has believed a lie. And you were born into darkness and deception.

My disobedience applies to all of us. Everything that I am, Mankind is. Everything I became at the Fall: fear-filled, materialistic-minded, applies to all of us due to the fact that you are all in me! You were in me at the Fall. Paul says to the church at Corinth, *"In Adam all die!"* [114]

The Body-of-Adam finds itself under the headship of Satan. When I submitted myself to the serpent, I gave over to Satan the authority over Eve, myself and all my responsibilities. I yielded my birthright to Satan. It's why Satan sees himself as the ruler over all the Kingdoms of the World. God had given that mandate to me. When Jesus was tempted by the devil in the wilderness at the end of His 40-day fast we read that He offered to Jesus all the Kingdoms of the World.[115] He sees himself as the ruler over the Kingdoms because he usurped my authority. The good news is that Jesus reclaimed what is ours through His obedience.[116]

In John 8, Jesus speaks to a group of Pharisees saying, *"You are of your father the devil, and you want to do the desires of your father. He was a murderer from the beginning, and does not stand in the truth because there is no truth in him. Whenever he speaks a lie, he speaks from his own nature, for he is a liar and the father of lies."* [117]

There are powerful truths here. Jesus describes them as belonging to one father as members of one body. There is no truth in Adam. The Body-of-Adam speaks lies. Every original truth from Heaven is distorted through a veil of lies twisting the creation into hideous fabrications. We act according to the nature of "our father" or "master" - the head of our Body. Our lives mirror the state of the master and Head of this Body. Jesus puts it this way in Matthew 10: *"A disciple is not above his teacher, nor a slave above his master. It is enough for the disciple that he become like his teacher, and the slave like his master. . ."*[118]

The Body-of-Adam is also known in Scripture as: "The Body of Flesh,[119]" "The Body of Sin"[120] and "The Body-of-Death."[121] These passages do not refer to our bodies as individuals, but to the corporate Body-of-Adam. All the members of this Body are "sinners" merely because they belong to the Body of Sin. I Adam, am the sinner.

To the church in Ephesus Paul says, *"You were dead in your trespasses and sins, in which you formerly walked according to the course of this world, according to the prince of the power of the air, of the spirit that is now working in the sons of disobedience. Among them we too all formerly lived in the lusts of our flesh, indulging the desires of the flesh and of the mind, and were by nature children of wrath, even as the rest."* [122] In Adam, we are all the sons of disobedience and children of wrath. We are an angry people!

The head of this body is Satan, but the heart of the Body-of-Adam is "Law." In my next lecture, I will explain Law within the context of Adam's Body.

The bottom line is that this Body is completely dysfunctional! It's members mirroring its head, living veiled to Truth, paralyzed by fear and driven by materialistic worship.

Summary

The following list summarizes the state of the Body-of-Adam in light of what I have shared with you so far.

The Body-of-Adam	
A.k.a: Body of Sin, Body of Flesh, Body-of-Death, Sons of Disobedience	
Our state:	Death
Our master/head:	Satan
Our identity:	Sinners
Our reality:	A distorted created realm of evil.
Our language:	Lies
Our motivation:	Carnal, sensual and material.
Our behavior:	Evil as a result of lies, fear and shame.
Our code/government:	The unholy trinity of legalism (see next lecture).

Chapter Eleven

I, Adam

Lecture No 11: I Am Legalism

> *"Law will take over because law always carries with it a sense of security and manipulative power."*
>
> Richard J. Foster

Welcome back! In my last few lectures, I unpacked some of the consequences of Eve's and my disobedience. Deception, fear and shame being the prominent ones. And, in my previous talk, I bundled all humanity into one corporate Body.

In this lecture, I want to help you understand the issue of Law and how it works in the fallen environment I created.

Please make yourself feel comfortable and if you can get me one of those coffees you've been serving yourself, I'd be very grateful. Thanks.

What Is Law?

To start with, we need to recognize that the Law of God is good. All Scripture, God's Word, and all His Laws are inspired and beneficial. Therefore, the problem with Law is not in the content of God's Law: *"The Law is holy, and the commandment is holy and righteous and good."* [124]

Law was necessary, but it didn't do anything to restore us to our relationship with God. Law couldn't rescue us from our orphaned state. It couldn't reinstate us to our original identities held in Christ. It was unsuited to awaken us to our song and voice. God didn't design the Ten Commandments and its associated precepts for those purposes. All it could do was attempt to bring some order into the chaos of the Adamic-referenced society!

Here's how Law operates within the Body-of-Adam.

As you read on, please bear in mind that I, Adam, am the Sinner. You are a sinner by belonging. It has become your identity. Sin, with a capital "S," introduced an Orphan spirit and caused all the evil we know in the world. When I mention "sin," I am less concerned about the behaviors than I am the about the brokenness that has embedded itself in your inner beings such as fear, lies and shame. It is my belief that Elohim concurs with my view.

The first thing about Law is that living in the Body-of-Adam has caused all of us to become focused on self-preservation in a darkened environment. You're all on a quest looking for a hypothetical needle in a haystack with seven other billion people. Love, truth and identity is humanity's Holy Grail that no one can recover within the Adamic Body. Consequently, we've developed a code by which we live – a Law so to speak – that governs our actions: The Law-of-Sin. I will refer to it as the Sin-Code and develop this issue first after introducing to you the other members of this unholy trinity.

Secondly, Eve and I established the idea, in the absence of spiritual consciousness, that knowledge of good and evil is the foundation for right living in the created realm. As a result when one breaks the social, moral code that emerged from the knowledge of good and evil, one is looked upon as having perpetrated an offense and is, therefore, guilty. Remember that love, wisdom and honor were always meant to be the criteria for right living in our original design - not knowledge of good and evil. The Law is a moral-code!

Thirdly, when Eve and I sinned we introduced a specific lie that embedded itself into the consciousness of Mankind: "God (or the gods) are angry; we need to appease them." They are our ultimate judges. So we invented all sorts of deeds, laws and traditions to abide by to satisfy God's righteous requirements and to justify ourselves. The law is a system of self-justification: a self-justification-code!

There it is! An "Unholy Trinity of Legalism," that has hijacked the good Law of God: the Sin-Code, the Moral-Code, and the Self-Justification-Code.

In brief: The social and legalistic system of the Body-of-Adam drives us, first of all, to behave "sinfully." Then, it accuses and judges us according to its unattainable moral-code manipulating us through guilty emotions to absolve and justify ourselves before God and peers because we regard Him to be an angry judge. God's Law is sound and beneficial, but, as the Apostle Paul says, sin took advantage of God's Law. My original sin turned Law into a system of guilt and condemnation.

Paul explains this to the church in Rome. He says, *"but sin took advantage of this law and aroused all kinds of forbidden desires within me! If there were no law, sin would not have that power."* [125]

Having introduced the three members of this unholy trinity, let's look at them in greater detail if you will!

The Sin-Code

Paul continues in his letter to the Romans: "For I know that in me (that is, in my flesh) nothing good dwells; for to will is present with me, but how to perform what is good I do not find. For the good that I will to do, I do not do; but the evil I will not to do, that I practice. Now if I do what I will not to do, it is no longer I who do it, but sin that dwells in me. I find then a law, that evil is present with me, the one who wills to do good. For I delight in the law of God according to the inward man._But I see another law in my members, warring against the law of my mind, and bringing me into captivity to the law of sin, which is in my members. O wretched man that I am! Who will deliver me from this Body-of-Death?" [126]

Observe the language Paul uses: I see a law in my members bringing me into captivity to the law of sin! Paul is describing the Sin-Code! Also, note Paul's final statement: *"Who will deliver me from this Body-of-Death?"* The implications are that the Sin-Code resides in the Body-of-Adam (aka the Body-of-Death) and motivates all its members.

Have you heard of Isaac Asimov's laws of robotics? Isaac Asimov was a prominent Sci-Fi author who pioneered the idea of intelligent robots serving human beings. To protect humankind from being harmed by the machines the following laws are hard-coded into each robot:

1. A robot may not injure a human being or, through inaction, allow a human being to come to harm.

2. A robot must obey any orders given to it by human beings, except where such orders would conflict with the First Law.

3. A robot must protect its own existence as long as such protection does not conflict with the First or Second Law.

Every robot produced is encoded with these three laws. A robot cannot violate these laws. Except, of course, that sometimes things don't always go as planned.[127]

The Law of Sin (or Sin-Code) is a governing social code written into the consciousness of the Adamic Body and has been developed to survive life and the chaos of The Body-of-Adam. It goes something like this:

1. Be the master of your life and destiny - only the strong survive!

2. Never yield control of your self-will & choices to another - trust no one!

3. Create your identity by yourself - seek success whatever the costs!

It's *The* Social Code of Fallen Humanity!

You can easily see the behaviors that emerge from its application. Control, works, unreasonable expectations, suspicions and distrust, an "ends-justifies-the-means" type of mentality, the survival of the fittest, selfishness, self-promotion...The list goes on and on.

This code governs everything you are and do in Adam: Your relationships with others, how you interpret the Bible, your view and relationship with God ..., the to-do list of your life..., your drivers to succeed! Everything!

In the Body-of-Adam, your sense of worth is ascribed to you by how well you apply the Sin-Code. This code is ruthless in enslaving us to its requirements. It keeps the members of "Adam" in bondage to fear. You worry because you can't control your destiny. You believe that everything you earn and possess are the result of how well you are in control of your lives. You fear loss because it means you're not in control!

That's the Sin-Code! The first "person" of the unholy trinity of legalism that governs the Body-of-Adam!

The Moral-Code and Its Enforcer

Back to Romans: *"Do you not know, brethren (for I speak to those who know the law), that the law has dominion over a man as long as he lives? For the woman who has a husband is bound by the law to her husband as long as he lives."*[128]

The Moral-Code replaced the original understanding Eve and I had, that right living flowed from aligning our behaviors to love, truth and honor in Christ. Knowledge of good and evil became our new reference for living right. But that caused a significant problem: we confused God's Laws with righteousness!

The Body of Adam is a virtual Police State. You have a personal valet, a resident prosecutor of sorts, shadowing you wherever you go. He never ceases to judge your actions against the Moral-Code, never missing an opportunity to accuse you every time you fall short. I refer to the resident accuser as a person with a name. Mr. Law, or to be more personal I've given him a first name - Lamont. If you are curious as to the choice of this first name, Lamont comes from the Scottish and means "Law-Man."

Lamont continuously forces you to perform to an impossible standard and condemns you when you fail. On top of that he always changes the terms of his expectations making it impossible for you to reach the standards. On one hand, you have the Sin-Code that you must live by to survive socially in the Body-of-Adam forcing you to do things you do not want to do. Then, you have Lamont with his Moral-Code accusing you every time you do wrong causing you to feel guilt, condemnation and shame. On top of that, he shifts the goalposts all the time. Lamont's Moral-Code takes its roots in the Tree of Knowledge of Good and Evil and has been manipulated to keep you in slavery.

While you are under Lamont's oversight, you will have to put up with the shame and guilt that comes from never being able to live up to his expectations. This man, being a righteous perfectionist who always knows what is RIGHT, incessantly makes you feel belittled, ashamed and guilty for not living up to "The Righteous" standard. He is relentless. He's an ugly piece of "excuse-my-French!"

While you're "alive" (in Adam) you're bound to Lamont like a wife to a husband. He is a self-righteous piece of work who abuses and disdains you, forces you to perform to an impossible standard, rejects you and then condemns you when you fail. The problem is that you can never let go of him!

The Sin-Code and the Moral-Code are constantly at odds. The Sin-Code demands success, stipulates selfishness, and encourages you to break the Moral-Code to establish your identity producing all sorts of evil and immorality. The Moral-Code finds fault in you for being selfish, lying and cheating to achieve your goals. Lamont belittles you and causes you to feel shame, guilt and condemnation. You need the Moral-Code to keep you in check, but you hate Lamont who enforces it for making you feel bad.

In a sense, because of your sense of guilt brought upon you by Lamont you have become severe and pitiless judges of one another and yourself. This moral code is not God's Law, but hijacks God's words, laws and requirements to blame and control us. While the Moral-Code is active, you have no choice but to be legalistic, critical, judgmental and even jealous. This is compounded by the Sin-Code, who places you in competition with all the other members of the Body.

Self-Justification

The Sin-Code is a system that drives us to behave sinfully, and then the Moral-Code accuses us (enforced by Lamont). So we find ourselves driven to justify ourselves before God (which we see as an angry Judge), ourselves and our peers. It is because Lamont accuses us that we seek to appease God. It is the Sin-Code that pushes us to do "wrong." It's a vicious cycle.

You might object by saying, “but wasn't Law given by God?” Yes, God gave us some law - the Ten Commandments for instance and many other useful instructions. But, both the Sin-Code and the Moral-Code hijacked the good Law of God and turned it into a means by which we feel we need to justify ourselves: A Self-Justification-Code.

While we insist on being in control of our lives in submission to the Sin-Code, we remain slaves to Lamont LAW, who continues to accuse us. Our sense of guilt forces us to obey the demands of the written and unwritten commandments in the hope we would absolve ourselves of our wrong.

Self-Justification looks different for each one of us. For some, it's very religious, as we want to appease God through our compliance with morality and good works. For others, it's self-improvement. Karma has become the in-vogue terminology: we want to ensure we have a positive balance of "good" to ensure good Karma comes our way.

It doesn't matter what we do to justify ourselves; it's still self-justification. We may not always overtly justify ourselves before God, but instead of God we might merely justify the ends by the means to shut Lamont up! It's still is Self-Justification. It's all religious! Religion is a tradition practiced in various forms within the Body-of-Adam since the beginning of time. We need to escape religion, not champion it!

Chapter Twelve

I, Adam

Lecture No 12: I Am Dead

"Unbeing dead isn't being alive."

E.E. Cummings

You Will Surely Die

Let's kick off this lecture with some Scripture:

"The LORD God commanded the man, saying, 'From any tree of the garden you may eat freely; but from the tree of the knowledge of good and evil you shall not eat, for in the day that you eat from it you will surely die.' "[129]

"One man opened the door to sin. Sin introduced (spiritual) death. Both sin and (spiritual) death had a global impact. No one escaped its tyranny. The law did not introduce sin; sin was just not pointed out yet. In the mean time (spiritual) death dominated from Adam to Moses, no one was excluded; even those whose transgression was different from Adam's. The fact is that Adam's offence set sin into motion, and its mark was globally transmitted and stained the whole human race."[130]

God made it clear to me that disobedience leads to death. Physically, I died at the ripe old age of 930.[131] Old in your terms, but in God's way of measuring time I died within the day I disobeyed.[132] It wasn't just I who died; I took the entire corporate body, "Adam," with me into death. The New Testament reveals to us exactly how "The Body of Adam" would effectively die. But the story doesn't end there and what follows my death becomes the beginning of a new chapter: a New Covenant with a New Man, a New Entity, a New Creation and a New Body.

Jesus' Death

Let's make it clear right now that Jesus is "Older Brother" - the second person of the Trinity - become flesh.[133] He is God incarnate living among us. As such, He emptied Himself of His divine prerogative[134] and modeled for us what it meant to be fully and truly man: a Son-of-God.[135] It would take forever to unpack every aspect of Jesus' death, so I want to focus on one matter that is important to understand.

Romans 5 says that, *"Sin entered the world through one man, and death through sin, and in this way death came to all people!"*[136]

Jesus was the second Man and the last Adam.[137] He was not me, Adam the 1st; he knew no sin[138], but he became "Adam" (stood in our stead) and became sin. He became a Son-of-Adam[139] and bore the likeness of "Adam" as a Son-of-Man.

He came to die a sacrificial death. Through His death as a Son-of-Man, the "Body-of-Adam" would die with Him. Death came because of me, and the entire Body is subject to it. Jesus came to die that death as "Adam" - as Us! He took upon Himself my offense and he even felt the misery of the misery of the orphan[140] for a moment on the cross. And, when Jesus died as "Adam," the Body-of-Adam and the entire system that it represents expired with Him. It is not the members of the Body that Jesus killed off on the cross; it is the Body as the container and the system of Law that governs it: The Body-of-Adam. Jesus became Adam, Son-of-Man and bore the likeness of Adam. He took on the Sin of Adam[141] to die as Adam so The Body-of-Adam might die and remain dead. When Jesus died, Adam died and with Him the Law system died including the Sin-Code, Lamont LAW our accuser and the need to justify ourselves... It all died in Adam when Jesus died! My original sin was buried in the grave with Jesus! It all got killed off once and for all!

"Adam" is dead, long live King Jesus! The old self is dead! The Body of Sin and Death is dead! Paul confirms it with these words: ". . . in this way death came to all people."[142] Think of it this way: the entire human race is in a spaceship. The ship is broken and heading for disaster. That's me, Adam - my Body! People are panicking, rioting, living in fear of their lives. A new vessel (Body) is built. There is room for everybody to step out of the old ship and into the new before the old disintegrates into oblivion. Jesus came to put the last nail in the dying coffin of "Adam"! It is finished. I, Adam am dead!

It's better than that, though. If you recall at the beginning of my previous lecture, I mentioned that all humanity existed in my loins when I walked the Earth at the beginning of time. Jesus died as me, the Adam that sinned at the beginning carrying all of humanity in himself. When Jesus died, I, Adam the 1st died, and you died in me. Therefore, you also died when Jesus died. I know it sounds complicated, but in simple terms: Jesus died and took the entire Body-of-Adam with Him into the grave!

Jesus' death as Adam didn't require you to perish. It means you've been dead all along. Dead Men in a Body-of-Death! Sin reigned in death![143] I, Adam, was dead from the moment I committed the Original Sin - and you were dead in me. Jesus came to make that death publicly known!

Jesus' death was the death of the Body-of-Adam - the death of all of us. His death is your death, but God's plan was so brilliant because it allowed the entire human race to develop and expand despite our sudden death in my loins at the beginning of our history. Remember that Older Brother, Christ, has kept your identities and purposes - God's Logos about and for you - in Himself since before I ever disobeyed. The blueprints of your lives have remained protected in Him. The killing off of the Adamic body gives you the opportunity to start afresh in His Resurrection. He rescued everything that was precious in my old dead body (that means the entire human race - every individual). And He discarded in the grave that which was useless and corrupted: that is, the Old Body-of-Death. Brilliant!

"Because God's children are human beings-- made of flesh and blood-- the Son also became flesh and blood. For only as a human being could he die, and only by dying could he break the power of the devil, who had the power of death. Only in this way could he set free all who have lived their lives as slaves to the fear of dying." [144]

The Sin Code is Broken

Everything the Body-of-Adam represents, the system that sustains it in it's morbid existence of death, it all got publicly nailed to the cross[145] and put down into the grave.

The Sin-Code is rendered powerless! When The Body-of-Adam died, confirmed by Jesus' death, the system that controlled us and forced us to act sinfully went to the grave with Him and stayed there!

Paul writes: *"I see a different law in the members of my body, waging war against the law of my mind and making me a prisoner of the law of sin which is in my members. Wretched man that I am! Who will set me free from the body of this death? Thanks be to God through Jesus Christ our Lord!"* [146]

There is another way out through Jesus Christ our Lord!

The Bad Marriage Ends

And, good news, the bad "marriage" with Lamont ends legally!

There is only one way for a dreadful marriage to end apart from divorce: that's when one of the partners dies. Lamont died with the Body-of-Adam. And in that death you died also! No need to divorce, the bad marriage is well and truly over! Everyone *is* dead!

Paul writes about that the church in Rome:

". . .do you not know, brethren (for I speak to those who know the law), that the law has dominion over a man as long as he lives? For the woman who has a husband is bound by the law to her husband as long as he lives. But if the husband dies, she is released from the law of her husband." [147] You are free, entirely free from Lamont's influence and control. Lamont is dead... but somehow his zombie still seems to speak from the grave!

The End

With the Sin-Code silenced and the accuser gone, we have no need to justify ourselves. We find that it is not God who seeks to judge and condemn us - Abba, Amma, and Older Brother welcome us home with open arms! At this stage, many of you are still living like dead men in a corpse, in bed with a dead husband who can't seem to shut up. It's chaos! It stinks too - smells like rotting corpses and there are zombie-like people everywhere! No wonder we live in fear of death!" [148] In death and fear! It's like the worst horror movie one can imagine. It's time to get out! It's all over people! I, Adam am dead. What are *you* waiting for to get out there?

Summary

Before closing this first series of lectures, I'd like to highlight fifteen "Big Ideas" covered:

1. God created us for Sonship and Rulership;

2. God designed us to relate to both the created and uncreated realms;

3. The physical mirrors the spiritual. Our physical bodies reflect our spiritual personas. The spiritual is the substance; the physical is a mere reflection of the spiritual.

4. God is the originator and architect of our identities. Abba and Amma are the progenitors of our spiritual personas. We are the expression of the Trinity's love. Older Brother carried and protected us in Himself; I, Adam bore your DNA in myself; I am the progenitor of your physical bodies.

5. Our soul is designed to process information and act in such a way that the will and way of Heaven become the reality on Earth.

6. We are Holy beings because God uniquely designed us among all creation, set us apart for a unique purpose, and we remained untainted by evil in Christ. God created us entirely free.

7. We are free moral agents: we can act freely upon our wills in an environment of unconditional love, uncontaminated truth, and God-blessed identities;

8. Maturity comes through the exercise of our will in obedience or disobedience to our Creators. Eve and I chose disobedience.

9. Love isn't forced upon us. Forced love is no love at all.

10. My disobedience "disconnected" us from the spiritual man in heavenly places, created a veil between Heaven and Earth, plunging us into a world of deception cut off from God. It blinded us from seeing our true selves in Older Brother tainting our vision of who we are, God, and the Cosmos around us.

11. Sin is Creation (as a free moral agent) saying to the Creator, "I do not need you." It is the son saying to the Father, "You are nothing to me." Everything else is the outworking of fear and lies.

12. Since my fall, Mankind is on a quest to recover that which was lost: Love, Truth and Identity.

13. All humanity is incorporated in Me (Adam) as One Body. It is the Body of Sin and Death. All died in me because of my sin.

14. Law governs the Body-of-Adam expressed as an Unholy Trinity of Legalism: The Sin-Code, The Moral-Code, and Self-Justification.

15. Jesus' death made my death final and public. The Body-of-Adam is in the grave, well and truly dead.

Part 2: The Second Adam

Chapter Thirteen

I, Christ

Lecture No 1: I Am The Resurrection

> *"Because God has made us for Himself, our hearts are restless until they rest in Him."*
>
> Augustine of Hippo

I am so delighted to have you with me for this second series of lectures. You cannot begin to imagine the joy and gratitude I feel. You are such a beautiful person. I am very pleased that we would meet today.

It was worth it all. *You* were *all* worth it.

Oh! You might be confused as to the change in lecturers today. Well, you see, your previous professor has been confirmed dead and won't make it to chair these talks of course. And since I'm not at all keen on resurrecting him, I felt it best that we keep him in his present condition. Excuse me if we don't feel too grieved about his passing. He was in a sad state.

Most of all, I wanted to do these talks. I felt I should have a heart to heart conversation with you. I don't speak for myself: I speak for Abba and Amma also. Our greatest desire is to open our hearts and minds to you. We don't want to be a mystery shrouded in the veils of religion.

So let me introduce myself to you if you haven't guessed by now. I am your Older Brother, Jesus, and you cannot begin to imagine the joy I have to share our thoughts and affections with you. I have some gifts for you hidden throughout the pages of these lectures. I hope you'll find them, discover and recover them. Please seek them and once you've found them, embrace and cherish them: they are your life! I have a voice and a song for you to sing. I hold the original blueprint of your life, identity, and authority in me.

I have a cloak of glory for you to wear too. Amma got it tailored to your specific measurements. And above all, the most precious gift of all, I want you to find and enjoy Sonship within us, The Trinity: a life of complete reconciliation and restoration. I hope you find these gifts. I want you to obtain them. We want you to shine because you are our beloved child.

Let's start our first chat.

Jesus Son of Man

I will start my story at my appearance on Earth.

I revealed myself on Earth clothed with an Adamic body incarnating the perfect Logos of God.[149] I bore all the features of Adam, yet without the deterioration caused by generations of degeneration engendered by lies, fear, and shame. My reference was Heaven, but my life was on Earth as the second Adam. I incarnated all the unconditional love of God, the uncontaminated truth, and a blessed identity: the complete Logos.[150]

Abba, Amma and I planned this course of action before we even created the Cosmos. I am the Lamb of God slain before the foundation of the world. I knew I would step into time and space to make my sacrifice known in your history.

I was compelled by our affections for you and came with a clear sense of purpose to display our love, reveal truth and reconnect you to your blessed Identity. I carried you in myself: not in a deteriorated form, but in the original unblemished state. Obviously this reconnection is only possible in a reconciled relationship with Abba, Amma, and I. I came to rescue you from the Body-of-Death and create a new safe place for you: a Body-of-Life. My death on the cross was the end of the old Body-of-Adam; my resurrection was the birth of the Body-of-Life.

Here's what happened. I was crucified and died carrying you and the entire human race in myself as Adam. I took over everything Adam was when He first disobeyed. When the Romans drove the nails into my wrists, they drove the final nail into the coffin of the Adamic Body. My death made Adam's death public and definitive. The Body-of-Adam has been humanity's coffin since Adam's original disobedience, but my crucifixion made it official!

I rescued and redeemed that which was precious in The Body-of-Adam: you, along with the billions of souls that were in Adam with you. The members of the Body-of-Adam were all sinners by virtue of belonging to Adam. They all "lived" in a darkened world, blind to their identities, yet reflecting the depravity of their own master, the devil, knowing only fear and shame, driven by a world of materialism. I've given to all of you a way out of darkness into light. We did this because we know who you are! We know your worth. You were not created to live in darkness, but to shine our glory.

Oh, It was indeed heartbreaking for Abba, Amma and Me to see you all living in this state of despair and brokenness. We desperately wanted you to know that you've always had a way back into the family. Yes, I was the Lamb of God slain before the foundation of the world. But this reality hadn't been announced yet. The world went about its business living in lies, fear and shame until the appropriate time in your history. It doesn't mean that it didn't break our heart to see you in this state. All parents and siblings suffer when the other members of the family are hurting.

The three days in the grave were critical. I didn't sleep during that time. I was busy preaching to spirits in prison.[151] There's no place we won't go to recover the dead. The time I spent in the grave is symbolic of the fact that it will take time for the Gospel to reach the moribund still doing "life" in the Body-of-Adam.[152] It'll take some time to transfer all the precious human cargo from the old dead Body-of-Adam into the new, resurrected body that I offer the World. That's if you accept the invitation and show up for the roll call of course; that's what we desire! You are all invited. All your names are on the roll. I sincerely hope not to remove your name out as an absentee.[153] But true love won't force itself: Abba, Amma and I can't violate the laws of love and self-will. It's up to you to show up.

In my parable of the Two Sons[154] the only person to miss out on the party was the son who never left Abba's house. He missed out because he was angry at Abba's extravagant grace, unconditional love and acceptance of the lost brother. It's not that he wasn't invited to the family reunion - it's just that the angry brother rejected the invitation. All humankind is invited to the party Abba has prepared for the homecoming of all the Sons-of-God in Me. Will you be angry at Abba's extravagant love and amazing grace? True love won't force itself!

On the third day, I resurrect from the dead. Amma came and breathed life back into my body just as life was breathed into Adam at creation offering a new genesis for Mankind. I rose from the dead presenting to you, to all humankind a New Body, a Body-of-Life, giving to all humanity a new Corporate Body to also rise into. I put to death the Body-of-Death as Adam and resurrected a new body, alive in the Spirit as Christ! Peter writes about me in his first epistle: *"For Christ also suffered once for sins, the righteous for the unrighteous, that he might bring us to God, being put to death in the flesh but made alive in the spirit,. . ."*[155]

I was always God-The-Son (the second person of the Trinity); I just want to make sure there's no confusion. As Older Brother, the second person of the Trinity, I never died. I can't. The second person of the Trinity can never be "separated" from the first and third person of the Trinity. The day a wedge is created between us is the day the Cosmos disappears. It simply will never happen because we are One God: Elohim!

I didn't die as the second person of the Trinity. However, it was the physical body I used to manifest myself in the created realm that died.[156] A body that was not conceived by humans, but begotten of God.[157] I came into this created realm as a baby born of a virgin.[158] I manifested myself as Son-of-Man (Adam). I was totally man, yet the manifestation of Older Brother: totally God.

The things witnessed and recorded regarding my life, death, burial and resurrection all pertain to my expression of life robed in the Adamic clothing (Son-of-Man). However, I need to point out that I always modeled what humanity restored and glorified (Sons-of-God) looks like in everyday life throughout my existence. The Gospels don't mention much about my formative years as a boy and a young man. They record my life on Earth for three years of ministry. But during my entire walk on Earth, I modeled your true identity and origin. I prototyped how life looks like as a Son-of-God. It was, however, in the sacrementalization of my resurrection that I made your original identity available to you. It's not that it wasn't available before - resurrection was always available in me as the Lamb of God - it's that you couldn't see what was available until I resurrected. The undeniable testimonies of my resurrection became the compelling call for all of you to step out of your deadness in Adam's grave and to embrace your life preserved in Me!

This New Body recovers something of primary importance, something Adam lost in the garden: a spiritual, glorious dimension with access to Heavenly realms! Paul writes to the church in Corinth: *"So also it is written, 'The first MAN, Adam, BECAME A LIVING SOUL.' The last Adam became a life-giving spirit. However, the spiritual is not first, but the natural, then the spiritual. The first man is from the earth, earthy; the second man is from heaven. As is the earthy, so also are those who are earthy; and as is the heavenly, so also are those who are heavenly. Just as we have borne the image of the earthy, we will also bear the image of the heavenly."* [159]

Remember how we created you? All of humankind was brought into the physical realm in Adam and into the spiritual realm in me - Older Brother - at once. Adam carried your physical DNA. I bore the original blueprints of your lives. The physical was the reflection of the spiritual into the created realm. Not only does the new resurrected Body-of-Christ create for you a new container in corporate terms (incorporating humanity), my resurrection awakens your spiritual body to Heavenly realms as well! You can now recover everything you lost in Adam's disobedience: Love, Truth and a Blessed Identity! You now have the opportunity and the means to step into your mature place as Sons-of-God within the family! You are alive in both realms in a new body I offer you in my resurrection. In Adam, you carried the image of the earthy! In me, you bear the image of the heavenly!

Here's another set of scriptures to contemplate:

"If we have hoped in Christ in this life only, we are of all men most to be pitied. But now Christ has been raised from the dead, the first fruits of those who are asleep. For since by a man came death, by a man also came the resurrection of the dead. For as in Adam all die, so also in Christ all shall be made alive.[160]

He is also head of the body, the church; and He is the beginning, the firstborn from the dead, so that He Himself will come to have first place in everything."[161]

...and from Jesus Christ, the faithful witness, the firstborn of the dead, and the ruler of the kings of the earth To Him who loves us and released us from our sins by His blood."[162]

The above passages mention that I am the first fruits of those who were asleep, the firstborn of the dead. It not only implies that I rose from the dead, but more importantly that I tasted death in the old coffin along with all of you. When I resurrected, I became a life-giving Spirit for all of you: I rose as the First Son-of-God; the first fruit of all the Sons-of-God. I was the firstborn of many Sons-of-God to come after me and to enjoy resurrection life in the corporate Body of Christ I offer humanity.

Jesus is Resurrection Life NOW

I will talk about how you can escape Adam's Body-of-Death as we move on. At this stage, I want to share some other valuable thoughts about my resurrection.

In the Gospel of John, chapter eleven, the author relates the story of the death of a dear friend of mine called Lazarus. I loved his entire family and often visited them. His sisters, Mary, and Martha, send for me because Lazarus is very ill. They obviously want me to heal him before it gets too late. But I had a better plan. I take my time and when I get to their place in Bethany, Lazarus is dead and has been so for four days. He's in quite a state of advanced decomposition by now. Martha is justifiably upset and interpellates me! *'Lord, if You had been here, my brother would not have died.'*[163] I chat with her. Try to calm her down. In our conversation I make this statement: *"I am the resurrection and the life; he who believes in Me shall live even if he dies, and everyone who lives and believes in Me shall never die."*[164]

I speak in the present here: "I am." I don't say, "I will be the resurrection and the life once they crucify me, and once I rise from the dead." I make it sure Martha knows that, right at this moment, and at every moment, "I am the resurrection and the life."

There has never been a time in the history of humanity where resurrection life in me has not been made available to you. I have been resurrection life since before the foundation of the world. I am the Lamb-of-God slain before the beginning of your history. I give life to you after death. Resurrection is my thing!

I declare that, "I am The Resurrection and The Life." "I am NOW – TODAY – your New Life" – not resurrection into the same old past but resurrection into NEW Life – I have kept for you the blueprint of the True You in myself. I have your song for you. This "You" has remained uncontaminated of lies, fears and shame. The blueprint of your innocence has remained unblemished in me. You don't need to relive the past; this identity needs to be discovered. In resurrection life, you learn the ways of the "Real You!"

In me, Christ, *Resurrection Today* is not a replicate of yesterday or a continuation of the past. It's the result of continuous death and resurrection in the One who IS ever Present in every NOW moment of your life. You can look forward to becoming everything we've spoken about you.

You can make a mistake today as you acquaint yourself with You! But I am always there as the I AM of your resurrection!

When you take your eyes off of the "I AM of Resurrection Life" it means you have to look into the past as your point of reference instead of the "I AM." The future will replicate the past if you take your eyes off the "I AM." What's more, the past and the future is a timeline of the Cosmos... your reference becomes the created realm rather than us, your Creators. You focus on the limited, rather than the unlimited, the degraded version rather than the original blueprint. And then you worry and panic!

In Me, Christ, the I AM, you can live in a continuous state of renewal, entering each moment into a NEW NOW of the Christ Resurrection Life I have on offer. Yesterday is dead. NOW is Resurrection Life in He who IS your resurrection and your Life: in Me, Jesus, your brother!

Lazarus needed to do one thing: heed the voice of Resurrection, calling him out of his state of death and decomposition into a new reality of Resurrection Life. That's all you need to do. Each moment you need to heed my voice, the voice of Resurrection calling you out of your old coffin of death into your continuous new state of Life.

The key to living in RESURRECTION LIFE is to heed my voice reminding you that you are IN ME. Stop listening to the voices from the grave and stay forever in the NOW of Resurrection Life. Your future is secure in the NOW of the I AM! In Me, Jesus!

"I am He who lives, and was dead, and behold, I am alive forevermore. Amen. And I have the keys of Hades and of Death." [165]

"Knowing that Christ being raised from the dead dieth no more; death hath no more dominion over him." [166]

Chapter Fourteen

I, Christ

Lecture No 2: I Am The Body of Life

"The temple of God is the holy people in Jesus Christ. The Body of Christ is the living temple of God and of the new humanity."

Dietrich Bonhoeffer
The Cost of Discipleship

I sincerely hope you have taken the time to let these lectures sink in. The purpose is not just to give you information, but rather to guide your pathway into reconciliation with Abba, Amma and Me so you can discover your original life in us. In that recovered life, you will know your destiny as a mature Son-of-God. I'm excited to lead you there. You are my reward. You, along with the many other brothers and sisters who step into this life.

In this lecture, I want to talk about My Body: the incorporated gathering of all those who have escaped the Body-of-Adam.

The Body of Christ

After the three days in the grave, I resurrect from the dead having vanquished all your foes and conquered all your fears. I rose as the champion of Truth, Love and Honor. In My resurrection, I created a new Body, The Body-of-Christ, for all humankind to resurrect into. You were dead in the old coffin of the Adamic Body, but I've given you the opportunity to resurrect into a New Body, a New Creation: The Body-of-Christ! My Body!

I, Christ, am the first fruits of all the resurrected; I am the One who died and resurrected from the dead. It goes to reason and remains undisputed that I am the head of the Body-of-Christ.[167]

Scripture uses other names to describe the Body-of-Christ: The Church, The Redeemed, The Spiritual Man and the Body-of-Life. All the members of My Body are Righteous by virtue of the One representing it: Me! In The Body-of-Life, you enjoy Fullness of Life! In this Body you are justified (no need for self-justification) and enjoy the abundance of grace and of the gift of righteousness.[168]

In me, you live in the NOW and The NEW of Resurrection Life!

Let's explore the ins and outs of the Body-of-Christ together.

Matthew 18 Commentary

Matthew Chapter 16 documents a crucial conversation I had with my disciples.[169] It's a foundational text for the Church. I query my disciples with this question: *"Who do people say the Son of Man is?"* I used "Son-of-Man" to describe myself instead "Son-of-God" because I wanted to refer to my humanity. I wanted my disciples to realize that I did everything in my humanity. The original Adamic robe was entirely human, but not deteriorated and dysfunctional.

Back to the story with Peter and the disciples, Peter replies, *"You are the Messiah, the Son of the living God."* In other words, "You are Christ, the one who liberates all people from the grips of death." No doubt Peter didn't see and understand the implications of "Messiah" in its full revelation, but that's beside the point. My messianic mission was to set the captives of the Body-of-Death free! Peter declares, *"You are the Son of the living God."* In that, he was right on the money.

"Although He existed in the form of God, (he) did not regard equality with God a thing to be grasped, but emptied Himself, taking the form of a bond-servant, and being made in the likeness of men." [170]

I was born a descendant of David according to the flesh and declared the Son-of-God with power by the resurrection from the dead![171] I came into this world and ministered to men as Son-of-Man and resurrected as The Son-of-God, first of many Sons-of-God to come after me. It means you are also given to arise into your original design as Sons-of-God in my Resurrection! It's what I've been claiming all along.

The word "declared" used in the English Bible in this passage (He was declared the Son-of-God)[172] comes from the Greek word "horizo." It means "to determine horizons." In My Resurrection, I defined the horizons (the boundaries) of authority and power for all the Sons-of-God to come after me. Immediately after My Resurrection I declared to the disciples that, *"All authority has been given to Me in heaven and on earth."* [173] The jurisdiction of your authority in my

Body-of-Life is limitless because the boundaries have been set in the unlimited spaces of the Heavenly realms!

Peter proclaims, *"You are the Messiah, the Son of the living God."* Then I explain that, *"On this rock I will build my church."* His statement is a rock; it's a foundational doctrine of Heaven's eternal strategy. It's upon this revelation (Peter's statement) that my Church, which is the gathering of all Sons-of-God in me, will be established. Think about it a little moment. I make an incredible promise to relocate humanity out of the Body-of-Death into my Body-of-Life. And I base that commitment on the fact that I, Jesus-Christ, am the Son-of-God! I did not intend to build the church by making people regret they are sinners or by preaching a fear of Hell - they are already in Hell!

The single statement that, "Jesus-Christ is the Son-of-God," is all I intended to use to gather the dead into life. Why? It's in your deadness that you can recognize your genesis and true identity in me, the Son-of-God. You see something of yourself in me. I, Christ, the prototype and the first fruit of the resurrected, offer hope for all the dead in Adam. I am the mirror of your true identity. And I know that getting a glimpse of your identity compels you. You see yourself in me. The dead in Adam, who have come to the end of their deadness and seek life, seek, in reality their true identity: that they are Sons-of-God. Peter's declaration rings in your ears as a call to Life - a call into your original identity.

Those who have already stepped out of death into life in me, the Son-of-God, repeat the message by reflecting their true origin and identity on earth as it is in Heaven. That's how I always intended to build My Church.

It's simple, powerful, profound and efficient! As you, Sons-of-God, acquire and acquaint yourselves with your original identity, your living in the Body-of-Christ reveals that I am the Messiah, the Son of the living God. The lives of Sons-of-God who live in their original identity speak more powerfully than words. And the gates of Hades swing open wide unable to keep its dead captive. *"The gates of Hades will not overcome it!"* The "it" I refer to here, is the Body-of-Christ, My Church (on this rock I will build my church). The gates of Hades is "the realm in which all the dead reside." Traditionally you've heard that Hades is Hell. This thought is misleading. The Body-of-Adam is "the residence of all the dead." What I'm saying is this: The Body-of-Adam will not be able to keep humanity in death. My offering of Resurrection Life, visible in the lives of all Sons-of-God, is irresistible to those seeking Life in their deadness. The gates of the Body-of-Death have swung wide open as the Good News message of Life calls all the dead into their original identities!

The Church

I resurrected from the dead over 2000 years ago. 2000 years since we - The Trinity in Unison - have began gathering together into my Body-of-Life the precious cargo rescued from the decomposing Body-of-Adam. 2000 years since people like you have been stepping out of death into life, resurrecting into the Body-of-Christ.

It all started with 120 disciples including the 11 Apostles in the upper room on the Day of Pentecost as recorded in the Book of Acts. About 3000 stepped out of death into life.[174] From there the Church kept on growing: steadily and miraculously welcoming into its bosom the lost, the least and the dead - restoring them to the Love, Truth and Identity. I have not stopped welcoming into My Body lost Sons-of-God since then. They have been found! They have discovered themselves in me! They have recovered their voices. Thousands upon thousands today are singing their songs of destiny in accord with Heaven. It's been rewarding and exhilarating to witness the revival of the dead in me!

What you often tend to forget is that the Church is not an institution. There's no doubt that institutions and organizations have become tools to promote my message. But institutionalized religion is not the goal. As a matter of fact, churches as institutions in form of local bodies or a global denominations have never been the point. The

Apostle Paul does a brilliant job in teaching that the Church is an organism called the Body-of-Christ.[175]

I know, it's not a new concept. But two millenary of tradition have developed a collective thinking that the Church is the organization, the things you do collectively, the traditions and beliefs you represent or even the worship service you attend. I think that you find it difficult to grasp what it means to be the Church as My Body.

I want to bring to the fore a thought that has been woven throughout this book since Adam's initial lecture. I want to highlight a fundamental, but powerful truth that naturally extends itself from the ideas developed throughout these pages. If the Body-of-Adam is the incorporation of all the dead in the history of humanity, then the Body-of-Christ is the incorporation of all the resurrected throughout the history of humankind. All those who have stepped into Resurrected Life in Me, Christ, make up a body that stands before the Godhead as righteous, redeemed and restored Sons-of-God.[176] That includes all the heroes of faith from the Old Testament, men and women throughout history who accepted by faith their resurrection in Me! Being a member of the body goes far beyond being a member of a local church, denomination or stream. It's bigger than that. When you resurrect into the Body-of-Christ, you become One with Me! I recovered for humanity the authority to rule and reign over the works of God's hands given to Adam in the first place. That authority was always yours in Me!

The Body-of-Christ is the Anti-[177]Adam. We are not against Adam! Adam is Dead! We replace Adam. And in replacing Adam, we have collectively, as One Body with Me at the Head, become humanity rehabilitated. The Body-of-Adam is humanity fallen. **The Body-of-Christ <u>is</u> humanity restored**!

The Temple

Buildings do not contain The Church. But the metaphor used in Scripture is that of The Temple. The Temple, as a building or container for worshippers, is a picture that describes the Body-of-Christ as a vessel assembling the Resurrected Ones in Me.

I was speaking to the crowd in the Temple courts on one occasion. In referring to the majestic and sacred structure, I proclaim, *"Destroy this temple, and in three days I will raise it up."* [178] Further on in the same chapter, John the author of the Gospel, writes: *"But He was speaking of the temple of His body. So when He was raised from the dead, His disciples remembered that He said this; . ._."*[179] The wording is clear: My Body (corporate gathering of the resurrected) is the Temple. It's not the Adamic clothing I incarnated that makes up the Temple; It's the incorporation of all the Sons-of-God throughout the ages who stumbled into resurrected life in me!

The original physical Temple made of stone was broken and destroyed by the Babylonians then rebuilt by Zorobabel. This refurbished version was still standing in Jerusalem, but had lost the presence of God and its Glory. The only thing that remained was law, traditions and a veil. It was a fitting representation of the Body-of-Adam in its glorious deadness. So I prophecy, "I will raise the Temple up! I will build another! My resurrected Body will become a Temple whose members fitly joined together live in the NEW and the NOW of Resurrection Life! I will gather worshipers in me as fully restored Sons-of-God who worship Abba in Spirit and Truth and live on earth as Ambassadors of Heaven." [180] The Gospels don't record my words exactly that way, but the intent was there!

The Love-Code

The Law that governed the Body-of-Adam is dead in Adam! Although many still try to do "life" according to the habits of the Old Body-of-Death. In The Body-of-Christ, you are totally free from the unholy trinity of legalism. Instead of abiding by the Old Law my people, are governed by the Law of the Spirit of Life. Romans Chapter 8 starts by saying that, *"There is now no condemnation for those who are in Christ*

Jesus. For the law of the Spirit of life in Christ Jesus has set you free from the law of sin and of death. For what the Law could not do, weak as it was through the flesh, God did." Sending His own Son in the likeness of sinful flesh and as an offering for sin, He condemned sin in the flesh. ._.[181]

This "New Law" is "The Love-Code;" it draws us into a life steeped in Heaven's values where its practitioners live from an awareness of love, truth and honor. Similarly to the Sin-Code, it is written and encoded into the fabric of the Body-of-Christ. Abba announced in Old Testament, *" 'This is the covenant I will establish with the people of Israel after that time,' declares the Lord. 'I will put my laws in their minds and write them on their hearts. I will be their God, and they will be my people.' "*[182]

The Love-Code is best communicated in a series of small statements I have developed for you below.

1. I am unconditionally loved and accepted by God: truth, love and honor crown my soul.

Therefore:

2. I choose to love God with all my heart, mind and soul: I am a free moral agent.

3. I love my neighbors and treat them with honor;

4. I love myself as I discover and live from my true identity.

Each of you can make these declarations and live by them because they become the law that governs life. Abba will keep drawing you into our love, truth and honor declaring your Sonship. Amma will keep encouraging you in this way. I will keep on walking beside you until this law becomes your default. Slowly this way of life will become your reality!

Here's how I summarize it best:

"A new commandment I give to you, that you love one another, even as I have loved you, that you also love one another. By this all men will know that you are My disciples, if you have love for one another." [183]

Summary

The following table summarizes the Body-of-Christ highlighting the main features of my Body.

<table>
<tr><th rowspan="2">"Parts" of The Soul</th><th rowspan="2">Functions of The Soul</th><th colspan="2">Functional Soul in Relationship with God</th></tr>
<tr><th>Divine Input: Logos</th><th>Harmonious Output: "Ruling Values"</th></tr>
<tr><td>Heart</td><td>Emotional</td><td>Unconditional Love</td><td>Peace</td></tr>
<tr><td>Mind</td><td>Rational</td><td>Uncontaminated Truth</td><td>Wisdom</td></tr>
<tr><td>Affections</td><td>Relational</td><td>God-Blessed Identity</td><td>Honor</td></tr>
<tr><td colspan="2">The WILL as outcome of processing our thoughts, emotions and affections</td><td>My Will is in Harmony with God's Will = Free Will (Freedom)</td><td>A Prosperous Soul = Prosperous Lifestyle & Healthy Body</td></tr>
</table>

Chapter Fifteen

I, Christ

Lecture No 3: I Am Your Life

"The resurrection completes the inauguration of God's kingdom . . . It is the decisive event demonstrating that God's kingdom really has been launched on earth as it is in heaven.."

N.T. Wright

Once again it is heartwarming for me to welcome you back to this next lecture. Make yourself comfortable. Can I tempt you with a latté and a chocolate éclair? I'm happy to prepare your coffee for you; I'm quite a barista you know. We source our coffee beans from a secret place. The best there is. This coffee is out of this world!

Let's get moving with this next lecture.

The Gospel Invitation

I want to talk about the Gospel invitation and the process of stepping out of death into life. Outside of me, you're all dead. I offer you your innocent life in My resurrection. That's the good news, The Gospel.

Let me give you a short definition of the Gospel:

The Gospel is Good News. The Good News is that Humanity is restored in Me! God is inviting humanity to step freely out of death into life and an eternal reconciled loving relationship with Himself as restored adopted Sons-of-God. It is a grace celebrated by a joyful declaration of faith in Christ.

Paul says, *"I am not ashamed of the gospel, for it is the power of God for salvation to everyone who believes, to the Jew first and also to the Greek. For in it the righteousness of God is revealed from faith to faith; as it is written, 'But the righteous man shall live by faith.' "* [184]

Grace

Grace is God's gift. Life in The Body-of-Christ and everything it involves is a gift. And it's simply free: *"For the wages of sin is death, but the free gift of God is eternal life in Christ Jesus our Lord."*[185] Remember the story of Lazarus in the Gospel of John? Lazarus was dead for four days in the grave. As a dead man Lazarus couldn't pay for his resurrection life. I called him out of his grave. As Lazarus was, so are you: dead! You are unable to pay for your new life. You can't arrange for your relocation. You might as well get used to the fact that there is nothing about obtaining resurrection life that you can achieve through your own efforts and merit.

Faith

Faith, in the context of new life, is simply your acceptance of my invitation into resurrection. It's an act of your will. You can't pay for this life because you're dead, so you simply need to accept it as a gift. Trust is not implied here either. A dead man trusts nobody. Faith, therefore, is also God's gift to you. It's God meeting those who have come to the end of their deadness and seek real life. Abba, Amma and I, meet seekers of life in their seeking and show them the way! We, the Trinity, believe you will respond.

But faith is also a confession, a declaration of faith in Christ, an acknowledgement of your lifelessness. It's a proclamation of hope! Above all, it's a recognition that I, Jesus, am the Son-of-God inviting you into your original Sonship! In his first epistle John writes, *"Whoever confesses that Jesus is the Son of God, God abides in him, and he in God."*[186] It's this confession that triggers your resurrection into my Body-of-Life.

From Death To Life

The process is quite simple in reality: you accept the Gospel invitation by faith. Something extraordinary happens at that moment. You find resurrection life. You escape the deadness of the Adamic coffin and resurrect into the New Life of the Body-of-Christ: alive in Christ. The veil is removed. Your eyes are opened (although it takes some time to get used to the light). And you begin to see who you are in Me: your true selves.

You resurrect from the deadness of the Adamic Coffin into an environment in the Body-of-Christ where you can be the person Yahweh always intended for you to be. In Christ, you have a name, an identity, a song that was always yours, but was veiled from you! Your new reference for living is Me, Christ and the life I've kept in myself for you - our Logos reserved and tailored just for you. You slowly become the incarnation of the distinct Logos reserved for you in Me! Slowly you will see yourself in Me and mirror that life on Earth as it is in Heaven.

When I was on the cross I saw you in the New Body - I envisioned all humankind that way - enjoying resurrection life. Being alive in My Body means that the Sin Code and Lamont Law have absolutely no jurisdiction over you. There is no need to justify yourself because you have been justified by my death. You are now born again - born into the Body-of-Life. You are alive in Me! And finally, one of the biggest things that with ever happen to you is that your Spirit-Man comes alive. A new incredible adventure begins.

"For you have died and your life is hidden with Christ in God." [187]

"Consider yourselves to be dead to sin, but alive to God in Christ Jesus." [188]

"You, however, are not in the realm of the flesh but are in the realm of the Spirit, if indeed the Spirit of God lives

in you. And if anyone does not have the Spirit of Christ, they do not belong to Christ."[189]

Alive, in Christ

You are alive in me! We'll talk about new birth in more details in my next lecture. Suffice it to say that you have made the right decision. But it's not the end of the journey. It's just the beginning. You have come into the blueprint of your life that is hidden in Me, My Body-of-Life! You are dead to sin and alive to Abba, Amma and Me! That's good news! Death, the Body-of-Adam, has absolutely no jurisdiction over you!

This passage from Paul's epistle to the church in Rome says it all:

"We were therefore buried with him through baptism into death in order that, just as Christ was raised from the dead through the glory of the Father, we too may live a new life."

"For if we have been united with him in a death like his, we will certainly also be united with him in a resurrection like his. For we know that our old self was crucified with him so that the body ruled by sin might be done away with, that we should no longer be slaves to sin--because anyone who has died has been set free from sin.

Now if we died with Christ, we believe that we will also live with him. For we know that since Christ was raised from the dead, he cannot die again; death no longer has mastery over him. The death he died, he died to sin once for all; but_the life he lives, he lives to God." In the same way, count yourselves dead to sin but alive to God in Christ Jesus."[190]

Many Scriptures describe what happens in Christ and who you *are* in Christ. To make my point, let me give a few passages to read:

"For you are all sons of God through faith in Christ Jesus. For all of you who were baptized into Christ have clothed yourselves with Christ."[191]

"Set your mind on the things above, not on the things that are on earth. For you have died and your life is hidden with Christ in God. When Christ, who is our life, is revealed, then you also will be revealed with Him in glory. . ._[192]

"For in Him all the fullness of Deity dwells in bodily form, and in Him you have been made complete, and He is the head over all rule and authority; and in Him you were also circumcised with a circumcision made without hands, in the removal of the body of the flesh by the circumcision of Christ.[193]

"He made Him who knew no sin to be sin on our behalf, so that we might become the righteousness of God in Him."[194]

"Therefore there is now no condemnation for those who are in Christ Jesus. For the law of the Spirit of life in Christ Jesus has set you free from the law of sin and of death. . ._[195]

". . . just as He chose us in Him before the foundation of the world, that we would be holy and blameless before Him. In love He predestined us to adoption as sons through Jesus Christ to Himself, according to the kind intention of His will, to the praise of the glory of His grace, which He freely bestowed on us in the Beloved. . ._[196]

"Therefore if any man is in Christ, he is a new creature; the old things passed away; behold, new things have come."[197]

As you acquaint yourself with the new you in the Body-of-Christ, you begin to live according to the new. It's an exciting place to be. Oh, you may fail once in a while as a child does. Have you ever seen a toddler stand up and master walking without ever crawling first? Do babies just get up and walk without ever falling? Of course not. You have a lot of learning about living according to the new. If you fail, it won't corrupt the blueprint! Abba, Amma and I will continue to teach and coach you into the fullness of your life.

You Are Loved

Here's one of the first lessons you'll learn in Me:

Abba, Amma, and I love you unconditionally in ways you could never even imagine. Our love and acceptance of you are entirely unconditional. We love you, and you can love us even if you've messed up your life. As a matter of fact, the Sin-Code, your ex-marriage to Lamont, the years of lies, fears and shame have messed you up. We don't care about how bad your life was. It's all dead and lies rotting in the Adamic grave. It's not that we don't care about you; we do, very much. However, your past life won't change the extent of our love for you. It doesn't bother us that, in your Adamic way of living, you were a prostitute, a murderer or a con artist. We are not disturbed if according to this earthly timeline you are addicted to drugs, porn or alcohol... or what your case may be! We are not afraid of your same-sex attractions.

I, Jesus, am not ashamed of you. Simply because I know you! Not the you in Adam, not the you of the present, past and future timeline! I don't see you according to the broken you. I regard you according to the innocent you, the particular Logos I carried of you in myself. I know who you truly are!

I will never say, "If you love me then you should be doing this and that. . ." I won't demand that you "go clean up your act first." I don't have conditions like, "You're safe as long as you keep your life under control. . ." And I don't place unrealistic expectations on you and then make you feel ashamed for not living up to them. As a matter of fact I won't lay down any provision, rule or expectation: Abba, Amma and I just love you – no strings attached.

The sole proviso - if you can call it as such - is this:

You must be dead to the Body-of-Adam, the Sin-Code, Lamont and Self-Justification. You must be completely and utterly lifeless to Adam's deadness. Your unconditional acceptance of Our unconditional love is solely based on you confessing that in Adam you <u>are</u> dead. And, since life in Adam is just that, death, you might as well accept the final blow. It's impossible to be "alive" to two reference points at once. You can't confess the old identity and try to apprehend the original innocent identity I've kept of you in me as well. Two identities in one skin make up for multiple personality disorders. That's not good!

When a child runs into his father's arms and declares, "I love you Daddy," the Father's heart melts. He will never say, "If you love me mow the lawn." When a father sees his children struggle, he won't reject them for not getting things right in life.

Children and parents are dead to any LAW when it comes to enjoying a loving relationship. . .Good Fathers make sure that love is not tied to any demands for performance or obedience. They refuse to bring law into love because the two can't mix.

You can't experience our love (the love of Abba, Amma and Christ) by figuring us out through the logic of the unholy trinity of legalism!

I died and then showed you the way to resurrection life. Resurrection life is not the old life revisited in a new skin. The process from Gethsemane to My Ascension is a model for you to follow. Remember my words? I declared, *"I am the resurrection and the life; he who believes in Me will live even if he dies!"* [198]

Since you *are* dead, there is no possible resurrection other than in Me. You accepted your death, burial and resurrected solely in Me, Christ. You cannot resurrect with the Sin-Code still alive. That's not possible. Neither can you continue to flirt with Lamont, unless you're into necromancy.

You resurrect into love, not law. Law and love don't mix. There's fear in law. I abolished law - indeed I destroyed it so you could resurrect through Me into love!

"For He Himself is our peace, who has made both one, and has broken down the middle wall of separation, having abolished in His flesh the enmity, that is, the law of commandments contained in ordinances, so as to create in Himself one new man from the two, thus making peace." [199]

"There is no fear in love, but perfect love casts out fear, because fear involves punishment, and the one who fears is not perfected in love." [200]

Returning to the old sin-code life is resuscitation. It's trying to keep a corpse alive, and too often you spend a great deal of efforts attempting to do that. Lamont Law will try his hardest to resuscitate the Sin-Code and to bring you back to himself. Once Lamont has reactivated the Sin-Code, your old zombie life will "revive", and Lamont will have you back in his deathbed.

Law will try to revive the old Sin-Code with words from the grave. "You're not praying enough! You don't have enough faith! You're not doing enough for God! If you love God, you would be doing more for Him! You should be offended at that! How can you worship God with those thoughts on your mind?"

Law won't let you live the Resurrected Life so quickly.

Your human sense of justice is only a reaction to law. Taking offense is only a response to law. You are hurt because somebody has offended your sense of right and wrong – the demands of law. Your insistence on "your rights" is only you kowtowing to Law.

You were dead in Adam. You are dead to the past. You have resurrected into Me, Christ. Don't bite the bait. Come on in, stay with Me, shut the door behind you and enter into your Family's abode! Let me introduce you to the rest of family. Abba and Amma just can't wait to meet you! They've prepared a feast to celebrate your arrival!

"Since you died with Christ to the elemental spiritual forces of this world, why, as though you still belonged to the world, do you submit to its rules?" [201]

Chapter Sixteen

I, Christ

Lecture No 4: I Am Your Identity

"My birth is imminent.

Forgive me, brethren.

Do not prevent me from coming to life."

Ignatius of Loyola

– As he faced the prospect of being devoured by wild beasts for his faith!

I feel we're making some headway together. I'm extremely pleased that you're committed. It's not just that you're devoted to listening to me. It's that you're attentive to the process and pathway I am leading you on. Your persistence and focus honor me. Just a few more lectures left and we're done, at least for the time being!

In this lecture, I want to unpack "New Birth" and the process of apprehending your innocent identity in detail.

Statements of Sons

When you come to the end of your deadness in Adam, I am there to meet you with the offering of New Life in My Body-of-Life. Your acceptance of this offering is the beginning of an amazing adventure. You accept my offer by faith.

New Birth is a process that yields some very clear outcomes. You will see the spiritual man awaken, recover your original identity in me and, above all, you will enjoy a restored relationship of true love in Elohim. All who know you will evidence the restoration of identity and the rousing of the spirit. It's hard to describe it as an event though: it's similar to a natural birth. Everybody knows a baby is born, of course, but try to look at it from the baby's point of view.

Pregnancy points to a coming birth. The fetus is unborn, yet a living being growing in the mother's womb.

Then there is the actual birth. For the baby, the process is not a one-time event. The baby becomes self-aware as a separate individual living among others over time. At birth, the baby is unaware. The baby doesn't even remember the trauma it went through to escape the mother's womb. Researchers suggest that there are five levels of self-awareness that unfold chronologically until the age of four or five. At that age a child knows it's an individual within a world of other individuals. Child psychiatrists use mirrors to determine a child's level of self-awareness. It's not until the child recognizes itself in the reflection that it realizes it has an identity apart from others. Then comes the long process of maturation into adulthood.

The point I am making is this. New Birth has various stages. It starts with receiving my Word as a seed where it remains in a state of "gestation." Then, there's the "event" where the person confesses their faith in me. A process of self-awareness occurs following this confession. The result is evidenced by the fact that the born again child has a definite sense of identity in My Body-of-Life. It's more than merely feeling "spiritually alive" or "saved," but the assertion of truths such as:

- "I am Son-of-God"
- "I am a Spiritual Being"
- "I am a Citizen of Heaven"
- "I am an Ambassador of God's Kingdom"

- "I exist to Reflect God's Glory" ("I do not live to reflect myself")

- "I am a Free-Moral Agent."

Awareness of these truths is just not enough; one must know the substance of these truths in their inner being. These declarations become alive and real. In a nutshell, this statement says it all: "**I am a Son-of-God in the Body-of-Christ born to reflect the Glory of God on Earth as it is in Heaven!**"

It's not a matter of salvation! I dealt with the issue of salvation long ago. You don't seek to assert these truths to be saved; you seek them because you are saved. I just wanted to make that clear!

Jesus' Chat With Nicodemus

A religious zealot named Nicodemus came to visit me one night. He said, *"Rabbi, we know that You have come from God as a teacher; for no one can do these signs that You do unless God is with him."* [202] What followed was an incredible conversation. I go straight to the heart of the matter: *"Truly, truly, I say to you, unless one is born again he cannot see the kingdom of God."* I steered the conversation where I wanted it to go. I wanted Nicodemus to understand that unless one recovers their original identity - the one lost by Adam - it's impossible to comprehend who you are in light of who I am.

The recovery of your original identity and design comes through the process of New Birth. I make it clear: "Unless one is born again he cannot see." New Birth takes you into the light where your sight is restored. It happens in My Body of Light. The Kingdom of God is first visible as your eyesight is restored. The veil is removed. Seeing is understanding. Vision gives you the desire and opportunity to apprehend that which you can see.

The point is this: at birth (the event of New Birth) you may or may not be aware of any noticeable changes. But the light is turned on, the veil is removed, and the conditions are right because you have entered My Body-of-Life. Your awareness is heightened, and you are on a journey into the realization of the New: into your innocent identity in God's Kingdom.

Before continuing commenting on this conversation with Nicodemus, we need to take a quick look at the Kingdom. Paul says that, *"The kingdom of God is righteousness and peace and joy in the Holy Spirit."* [203] Righteous is your justification before God in me, Jesus. You are righteous in the Body-of-Christ because I am the head of the Body - you are no longer "sinners" in the Body-of-Adam trying to justify yourself to the old Lamont Law. Righteousness is your "status" before God ! Peace is the harmony of your restored souls as you encounter unconditional love, know uncontaminated truth and reconnect with your blessed identities. Joy in the Holy Spirit is the outcome of restored relationships in community with the Trinity and others. That was just a brief definition of God's Kingdom. There's lots more to explore of course.

Back to Nicodemus

Nicodemus asks another question, *"How can a man be born when he is old?"* To that, I reply, *"Truly, truly, I say to you, unless one is born of water and the Spirit he cannot enter into the kingdom of God. That which is born of the flesh is flesh, and that which is born of the Spirit is spirit."* As you recover your vision and adjust your sight to life and light, you begin to apprehend that which you can see: the Kingdom. In "the flesh," the Body-of-Adam, the Kingdom is impossible to grasp because you are blind, and your spirit man is dead. New Birth is triggered by the awakening of your spiritual being by which you gain restoration of spiritual sight.

Slowly your eyes adjust to your spiritual realities. And you begin to acquaint yourselves with your true selves in Me. You start to enter into the substance of righteousness, peace and joy in the Holy Spirit. Your soul begins to sing a song of joy!

Nicodemus is confused. *"How can these things be?"* And I reply: *"If I told you earthly things and you do not believe, how will you believe if I tell you heavenly things?"*

The spiritual self, in Me (The Body-of-Christ), cannot be seen and understood by earthly reasoning. It must be understood and apprehended in the uncreated realm through spiritual eyesight. You must have your spiritual being alive to begin to understand this. The aha moment of Sonship, the "I am born again" moment is about to spring upon you. My prayer and will is that you enter into your spiritual dentity as you read these lines. That the unveiling occurs as you see who you are from a Heavenly perspective in Me.

Here, I give Nicodemus a powerful clue as to the makeup of the New Man: *"No one has ascended into heaven, but He who descended from heaven: the Son of Man."* I am revealing My identity to Nicodemus. I'm saying, *"This is who I am; I am as Adam was before the Fall; I am both physical and spiritual; I ascend and descend at will. . . Once you are born again, you will see who you are too! Alive to both realms."*

What a powerful conversation.

All Things Are New

New birth means you are born into the new! I am the New Body. In the Body-of-Christ the Real You - The Spiritual Self - is revealed to you. Who you are in Me becomes evident. What you will discover is that there is a dissonance between the old default Adamic reference of "living" and the new identity you are beginning to embrace. It's normal. The old is no more your norm. Adam is not your reference, but it has been your default all your life. Don't panic at the seeming enormity of the challenge: we, the Trinity, as one, will walk you into your identity. It won't come without trials and struggles. The Kingdom of God is revealed through much tribulations. [204] It's an incredible challenge to face your fears, dismantle the lies and overcome the shame that have accumulated in you over time and through previous generations. Your determination to seize the new must be unwavering.

You cannot compare the new to the old, except that you retain the memories of your old life. I feel the need to add that there are things in the old that become ingredients, the dust so to speak, that come together for good in the new.[205] The good and the bad of your past combine to set you free into your New Identity. There's nothing to regret about your past.

"Therefore if anyone is in Christ, he is a new creature; the old things passed away; behold, new things have come." [206] You are a NEW person in Me. The original blueprint of your life that you've never previously been introduced to is placed before you. As you acquaint yourself with the spiritual man, who is formed for the same purpose and of the same stuff as Me, Christ, you begin to mirror your true self. This "You" is shaped into your life on Earth as it is in Heaven. You discover this identity in me, Christ, and you re-educate your lifestyle to suit the new. You uncover who you are by focusing on the promises of the NEW YOU. This NEW YOU mirrors me! It is our Logos tailored just for you. It's your song, your part in the Symphony of History. We created you for this.

Look in the Mirror. Look into Me. What do you see? The Old Or The New?

Everything I, Christ, am, your spiritual man is. Everything your spiritual identity is, you become on Earth, not by forcing yourself to change the old, but by allowing us, The Trinity, to shape your physical being. You discover your true self and adjust to the new. Your thoughts, your beliefs and attitudes are transformed by the vision you have of yourself in Me. Your life slowly reflects the reality as you focus on the new.

If you say, "I am a sinner saved by grace," you are still living according to an identity steeped in sin: your life will reflect that. Your sin-consciousness and shame-consciousness keep you anchored on the old with guilt and condemnation ruling your life - sounds a lot like the old Body-of-Adam. The more you focus on the true self, the Christ-like you, the more you realize how loved and worthy you are in Elohim's Eyes. You see yourself the way We, The Trinity, have always seen you. The new you is just, holy, affectionate, able, patient, good and fearless.

What is your reference: the OLD in the Body-of-Death? Or the NEW in the Body-of-Life? Where do you get your identity from? Death or Life? Shame or Honor? Who is your model? The Adamic or Christ? The evidence of new birth is that your life will mirror the Christ-You as you declare, "I am Son-of-God!"

Everyone incarnates words! Either you embody the cursed words of lies, fear and shame spoken to you. Or you live God's particular Logos for you. The difference between the two is one confession away.

Turn your sights to Me! Keep your eyes on Me, Christ. Focus on the new. Then you will reflect on Earth, in your everyday living, who you are in Heavenly places. The author of Hebrews encourages us to, *"Keep our eyes fixed on Jesus the author and completer of our faith."*[207] In doing that you will come to that point of exclamation: "I am a Son-of-God!" You will enter the substance of everything I am! Your "I am" will reflect the "I am" words Abba, Amma, and I have whispered to you.

This next passage says it all: *"But we all, with unveiled face, beholding as in a mirror the glory of the Lord, are being transformed into the same image from glory to glory, just as from the Lord, the Spirit."*[208]

Your behavior will reflect what you see in the mirror. Your living will reflect the Logos we have declared about you in Christ as you align yourself with those words. Look at yourself in the mirror of Christ and declare who you are. Go on, do it!

James says, *"Prove yourselves doers of the word, and not merely hearers who delude themselves. For if anyone is a hearer of the word and not a doer, he is like a man who looks at his natural face in a mirror; for [once] he has looked at himself and gone away, he has immediately forgotten what kind of person he was. But one who looks intently at the perfect law, the [law] of liberty, and abides by it, not having become a forgetful hearer but an effectual doer, this man will be blessed in what he does."*[209]

Son-of-God

This whole thing is only possible as the Spirit of God (Amma) speaks to your spirit. Paul says: *"The Spirit Himself testifies with our spirit that we are children of God."* [210] Be attentive!

In closing this lecture I want to share a paraphrased version of Romans 8:15-17[211] that reflects many of the truths you've learned in this book:

Those who are of the Body-of-Adam set their souls and minds on the physical realm, the material, the created. But those who are alive in spirit within the Body-of-Christ set their minds and hearts on Heaven. For the soul set on the created realm is dead (in the Body-of-Death). But the soul set on the_spiritual realm finds resurrection Life and lives in peace. He knows peace, wisdom and honor. He lives a prosperous lifestyle. It's because the mind set on the created realm is opposed and closed to the knowledge of Elohim. Such people cannot live according to the Love-Code in Christ - they cannot do so. That's why they cannot please God.

However, you are not in Adam but are alive in Christ; if indeed you have stepped into resurrection life. If your spirit is not alive by the Spirit of Resurrection Life in Christ, you do not belong to the Body-of-Christ. If Christ is in You and You are in Christ, the old body is dead because of sin, but the new spiritual body is alive because of righteousness. If the Spirit of Resurrection dwells in you, that same spirit resurrects you into the new Body-of-Life.

So we are no longer under any obligation to live according to the demands of the Body-of-Adam and the unholy trinity of legalism - in that old Body-of-Death; you are dead. But if you resurrect in the new and discard the old in the coffin of Adam's deadness, all the ways of the old yield themselves to the new ways of life. All those who are alive in the Spirit are Sons-of-God. You are no longer slaves to the old and shrouded by the spirit of fear in Adam. You have received your adoption in God's love that casts out all fear. You cry out, "Abba - you are my Father." Amma testifies to that truth deep within your spirit. That's how you know you are a Son-of-God and indeed an heir of the Kingdom - co-heirs with Older Brother. You are glorified in Christ's Resurrection since you have identified yourself with His suffering for You.

Are you ready to make that declaration? "I am a Son-of-God!"

Chapter Seventeen

I, Christ

Lecture No 5: I Am Your Baptism

"Because the Christian God is not a lonely God, but rather a communion of three persons, faith leads human beings into the divine communion. One cannot, however, have a self-enclosed communion with the Triune God- a "foursome," as it were-- for the Christian God is not a private deity. Communion with this God is at once also communion with those others who have entrusted themselves in faith to the same God. Hence one and the same act of faith places a person into a new relationship both with God and with all others who stand in communion with God."

Miroslav Volf

-- *After Our Likeness: The Church as the Image of the Trinity!*

We've learnt a lot over the past four lectures. I hope you've given yourself the time to assimilate everything we've discussed. Embrace the process, but don't rush it!

Here are some of the key ideas:

- In My resurrection, I created a new corporate body to replace the dead Adamic Body.

- I offer you to step out of the Body-of-Adam to find refuge, restoration and real life in my Body-of-Life.

- Resurrection life gives you a new reference for living: instead of yesterday you can focus on the NEW today, instead of the broken shame-filled identity you can align your being to the Christ-like Identity!

- The Body-of-Christ, the Church is humanity restored.

- In Me, you learn to live in the Identity, the Logos we, the Trinity, have preserved for you.

- New birth is a process that leads you to declare, "I am a Son-of-God!"

This lecture may be a little longer than the others. I hope to make it all as concise and clear as possible. Sit back and take your time!

Before commencing My ministry, I met my cousin John by the Jordan river, and I asked him to baptize me. At first he didn't want to. He felt I should baptize him. After my insistence he accepted. We waded into the river, and he baptized me. Amma came and settled on my shoulder in the form of a dove. It's surprising the forms she likes to take!

Abba spoke saying, *"This is My beloved Son, in whom I am well-pleased."* It was a marvelous family moment. [212]

New Covenant Scripture talk a lot about baptism. When we see the word "baptism" in the text, we immediately think of the act and the ceremony. We imagine a group of people near a river, at the beach or by a swimming pool and some of them getting dumped into the water by others. You get that picture from my baptism by John. It's good and right to follow the sacramental act, but you must not forget the realities the act points to. Observances, teachings, doctrines and beliefs all guide you to substance.

There are astonishing ideas represented in the physical act of baptism. Remember that a sacrament is an event that is commemorated on Earth corresponding to a reality that has been sealed in Heaven. Baptism represents leaving the old and entering into the new.

Middle Eastern cultures and traditions understand this. When one is baptized into the Christian faith, it means a total forsaking of the previous faith and life. John-the-Baptist practiced baptism with the idea that the public statement of baptism showed a willingness to pass into a new thinking about life and God: the baptism of [213] metanoia.

The Apostle Paul advanced the idea of baptism being the act of passing from old to new. He postures that, in baptism, you identify yourself with my death, burial and resurrection. You move from the old to the new.

For instance, he writes to the Romans, *"Do you not know that all of us who have been baptized into Christ Jesus have been baptized into His death? Therefore we have been buried with Him through baptism into death, so that as Christ was raised from the dead through the glory of the Father, so we too might walk in newness of life. For if we have become united with Him in the likeness of His death, certainly we shall also be in the likeness of His resurrection, . . ."*[214]

And then to the Colossians he says that, *"In Him all the fullness of Deity dwells in bodily form, and in Him you have been made complete, and He is the head over all rule and authority; and in Him you were also circumcised with a circumcision made without hands, in the removal of the body of the flesh by the circumcision of Christ; having been buried with Him in baptism, in which you were also raised up with Him through faith in the working of God, who raised Him from the dead."*[215] Notice all the "in Him" statements in the passage?

A deeper reading of the Pauline writings seems to reveal a deeper understanding of baptism. This revelation displaces the traditional act into the background and brings to the forefront the ideas developed in our previous lectures. You are baptized into the Body-of-Christ. It is more than a traditional act. The act points to substance - a reality: you now belong to humanity restored. You are baptized into The Body-of-Christ made available to you in my resurrection. It's about your resurrection into my body following your immersion into everything that I am!

That truth leads to the second big idea highlighted in the word "baptism" itself. It represents being immersed in a substance that transforms the nature of the body being immersed. It's like making pickled onions. The vinegar solution transforms the onion into its flavor and characteristics.. [216]

Once you are baptized into my Body-of-Life, you cannot remain as you were. The old default thoughts, affections and behaviors will be displaced by the flavors and savors of My character. The Body-of-Life will transform you. It's important because the characteristics of my person are the foundations of your Identity in Me.

In this lecture, I want to explore various "environments" - "baptismal tanks" so to speak - in which particular works of transformation occur in your life.

- Your baptism into Me, Christ, as an environment in which you become like Me;

- Your baptism into the bosom of The Trinity as the setting where you experience our presence, love, goodness and affections. It's also the place you hear our Voice speaking the Logos of your life to you. It's where you learn our values;

- Your baptism into the community of faith as a representation of life in The Trinity;

- Your baptism into the Spirit as a means for the development of your spiritual being;
- Your baptism into our Word as your source of truth.

These five environments are conducive to total transformation, restoration and maturity.

Don't get me wrong, there is only One Baptism! *"There is one body and one Spirit, just as also you were called in one hope of your calling; one Lord, one faith, one baptism, one God and Father of all who is over all and through all and in all. . ."* [217] That single baptism - the one transfers you out of the Body-of-Death into the Body-of-Life - opens the door to a total transformation of your being: spirit, soul and body. Your spirit comes alive and is ignited to supernatural life. Your soul is healed and restored to peace and harmony in a place of unconditional love, truth and identity. You are transformed, or should I say regenerated into the fullness of your original makeup and design as I modeled to you while I lived in the flesh.

Why don't we explore those five environments together?

Your baptism into Me!

"For by one Spirit we were all baptized into one body, whether Jews or Greeks, whether slaves or free, and we were all made to drink of one Spirit." [218]

We've covered this thought extensively throughout previous lectures. When you accept my invitation into Resurrection Life, you resurrect from the deadness of Adam to life in the Body-of-Christ. Everything I am, you become.

In the new, you are transformed into my likeness. You become Christ-Like. You take on the substance of my nature. The Christ-you is revealed, and you mirror me on Earth as I am in Heaven. In practical terms, you focus on me, Christ, the author and completer of your faith[220] as the image of your true glorious identity[221]. Centering your thoughts on Me is like remaining submerged. You immerse yourself into this picture and acquaint yourself with who you truly are in Me. It's a determination in your hearts to become like Me, in My Body-of-Life.

Your baptism into the bosom of The Trinity!

"For you have died and your life is hidden with Christ in God." [222]

"For Christ also died for sins once for all, the just for the unjust, so that He might bring us to God, having been put to death in the flesh, but made alive in the spirit." [223]

You are in Me, and I bring you to the Trinity - I hide you in Us! I, Jesus take you into myself and accompany you into the bosom of your Heavenly family where you experience unconditional love, know uncontaminated truth and come alive to your blessed identity. You experience communion with us, in our presence. You are included in us. We share our desires, will, affections, wisdom, compassion, goodness and love with you. And you begin to live totally loved on Earth as you are in Heaven. You enjoy peace that surpasses all understanding and joy unspeakable and full of Glory.

The word "bosom" talks about the place of loving care and protection. Abba's, Amma's and My affection, love and passion for you is indivisible. The fire of our passionate love burns for you deep in our heart.

Knowing us this way is Eternal Life. When I prayed to Abba in John 17, I say this: *"Now this is eternal life: that they know you, the only true God, and Jesus Christ, whom you have sent."* [224] Then later on in the same chapter I continue saying: "*That all of them may be one, Father, just as you are in me and I am in you. May they also be in us so that the world may believe that you have sent me."* [225] It's my prayer that you would abide in Us! To know the goodness and heart of Elohim cannot leave you unchanged. To dwell in our presence is an experience without parallel. You will always want to return to that place.

David, the shepherd, psalmist and King knew Elohim; he knew that place of intimacy with Us! That's why David has a special place in our heart: *He (God) testified concerning him (David): "I have found David son of Jesse a man after my own heart; he will do everything I want him to do."* [226]

In our Bosom, you begin to identify yourself with the values of The Trinity such as love, honor, joy, peace, servanthood, creativity and wisdom just to name a few.

Prayer and praise in our midst and with us, not to us, is a practice that keeps you immersed in our presence. Praying to us keeps you at a distance. Praying with us keeps you centered in our midst!

Finally, there is one more thing that you will experience in our bosom. You acquaint yourself with our voice. We speak and sing over you. We reveal our plans and thoughts for you. We share with you the details of your blessed identity. Slowly you will align your life with our thoughts. Truth displaces all the lies. Love banishes all the fear. Honor overcomes all the shame.

Your baptism into the Community of Faith!

Baptism into my Body-of-Life comes with an interdependent interconnected association with all the other members of my Body-of-life. My Body is The Church. It is humanity restored, the incorporation of all the Resurrected Ones, who follow in my footsteps and accept to pass from Death to Life in Me.

You are baptized into Me. Then, I accompany you into the Bosom of The Trinity - The Presence. You learn the heart, thoughts and ways of The Trinity!

However, the values of the Trinity are expressed and lived out in community. That's where the local body of like-minded disciples learn to live the ways of the Kingdom on Earth as they are in Heaven. Notice that community flows out of the presence. It is very difficult to enjoy community if one ignores the presence.

Discipleship calls you into a realization of your identity: “I am Son-of-God”! And then it guides through the process of transformation. The context in which this discipleship occurs is a community of believers. In the local community of faith you come to the realization that you are a Son-of-God. You learn to live in your God-blessed identity. You begin to understand and live the ways of the Kingdom of God to live in real freedom. You discover your part in the Kingdom as a Son-of-God and are released into your destiny so that the Kingdom of love might invade Earth.

You do not achieve this as an individual in isolation of others. It develops within the context of the local community of faith. Fathers of faith lead such communities. They create a prophetic environment where the values of Heaven are enjoyed. Fathers know how to release Sons and Daughters into their blessed identities. They recognize your gifts, speak blessings and champion your place in the Kingdom. You learn to explore and exercise your faith and authority. It's exciting to do life in such an environment of freedom and growth. The local community of faith is a baptismal tank where we learn to live the values of The Trinity. Find one and immerse yourself into the waters of community!

Your baptism into Spirit life!

One of the highlights of my Church's inauguration in Acts is the event known as the "Baptism of the Spirit." The story goes like this:

"When the day of Pentecost had come, they were all together in one place. And suddenly there came from heaven a noise like a violent rushing wind, and it filled the whole house where they were sitting. And there appeared to them tongues as of fire distributing themselves, and they rested on each one of them. And they were all filled with the Holy Spirit and began to speak with other tongues, as the Spirit was giving them utterance."[227]

The Apostle Paul expands on this event and explains that there are more "Gifts" of the Spirit at work within My Body. You can read about it in 1 Corinthians 12. [228]

In Adam's first two lectures of this book, he explains how we were created with two "bodies" (a spiritual body, giving us awareness of the Heavenly (uncreated) realm, and the physical body giving us an appreciation of the physical (created) realm). Adam lost the spiritual dimension; he cut you off from the Heavenly; your spiritual bodies lie dormant in Me, awaiting resurrection. I lived on Earth modeling this way of living. Remember my words to Nicodemus? *"No one has ascended into heaven, but He who descended from heaven: the Son of Man."* [229] They are an accurate description of the fact I could access Heaven and Earth freely.

The Spiritual Man can see, hear, touch, smell, talk, move in Heavenly realms just as your Spiritual Body does in the Physical dimension. It is designed to gather information and to send the information to your Soul.

The Pentecost event is significant because it points to the awakening of your spiritual body. Your spirit awakens in Me. One of the first supernatural "things" you may learn to do naturally is to speak in a Heavenly language. The spiritual body can do more than speak in Heavenly languages, though. It can see (visions, dreams and prophecy); it can manipulate the physical (signs and wonders); it can taste and feel the substance of Heaven. I modeled that for you while I lived among you. The Gospels tell the stories of my miraculous works. Paul's list of gifts points to the fact that there are an unlimited amount of abilities given to your spirit that empower you to do God's will on Earth. However, just as the physical becomes weak and even loses its abilities without exercise, the spiritual needs to be built up and applied.

Speaking in tongues, when exercised, becomes a supernatural thing you do naturally at will. There are hosts of other things your spiritual bodies can do as you seek them and apply yourself. Speaking a Heavenly language points to a greater truth. You are first a spiritual being, and I recovered that for you in My Resurrection. It is your responsibility to exercise yourself in the realm of the Spirit; to remain immersed in the Spirit and to acquaint yourself with your spirit man's "gifts." Eventually, you will exercise the supernatural as naturally as everything else you do.

Your baptism into God's Living Word!

Let's read a few passages of Scripture to start with:

"Therefore no one is to act as your judge in regard to food or drink or in respect to a festival or a new moon or a

Sabbath day-- things which are a mere shadow of what is to come; but the substance belongs to Christ."[230]

"Now faith is the substance of things hoped for, the evidence of things not seen."[231]

Faith celebrates as certain what hope visualizes as future."[232]

". . .Do you want to know, O foolish man, that faith without works is dead?"[233]

"Hey man, if you have nothing to show for your faith your faith is meaningless; it remains a dead doctrine."[234]

Let me bring it all together into a coherent thought! Faith brings belief and hopes into reality, into a substance: Me, Christ! Without the "coming into substance" of your hopes, beliefs, and indeed your doctrines, your faith has produced nothing, it is dead - useless! It means that **faith is an active pursuit of entering into the substance of the Logos - God's particular thoughts for and about you**.

In a previous lecture, I mentioned that faith is "acceptance of my offer of new life." Once the gift is received, you become active in pursuing the reality of everything I am! The acceptance of the gift must be followed by the pursuit of the fullness of the gift and what it means. Resurrection life is not a passive one.

The end game of all doctrine is to know Me, Christ! It's to encounter everything that I am because I am the image of the invisible God[235] and all the fullness of the Godhead dwells in Me. [236] But it goes further: Everything that I am you become. God sees you in Me. And in Me, Christ, you become like Me in the reality of everyday living. Faith takes you there: into the substance of who I am and living in that reality transforms you. It is a real immersion into me, a baptism that transforms. If doctrine doesn't take you into substance, then you are like an unfertilized egg that has been placed in an incubator and eventually hatches nothing but rottenness.

Many claim that Scripture is their only source of truth. They assert that the Bible is their only authority for doctrine and conduct. That's good. But without spiritual insight, revelation and restored "sight," the understanding of the Bible remains limited to human interpretation. The Bible is your only source of truth for doctrine, teaching, lifestyle and conduct, but it must be interpreted with spiritual and Heavenly insight. And most of all it must take you to a place where you hear the voice of the one who spoke the Word in the first place. Access to wisdom from above is in God's Word - The Bible. And transformation comes as a result of understanding and applying its truths as it leads you to the Author. A Son-of-God is a student of God's Word. A Son-of-God remains immersed in God's Word and the outcome is transformation and wisdom. But most of all, Scripture must guide you to the voice of God, the one who represents the Logos (I, Christ!) and into the reality it represents!

Proverbs 2 says: *"For the LORD gives wisdom; from his mouth come knowledge and understanding."* [237] James says, *"But if any of you lacks wisdom, let him ask of God, who gives to all generously and without reproach, and it will be given to him. But he must ask in faith without any doubting, for the one who doubts is like the surf of the sea, driven and tossed by the wind."* [238]

Close

In Me, Christ, your spirit-man comes to life. You see and learn to live in your blessed Identity. The veil is removed. You see again. You are in the light. In the Trinity's bosom, you experience our incredible unconditional love and acceptance.

In God's Word, you have access to unlimited, uncontaminated truth. You can apply wisdom from above to your decision-making process as you align your thoughts with Heaven. The result is that your free moral agency is restored. You are at peace, in harmony. You can participate in doing God's will on Earth as it is in Heaven within a community of faith.

Remember this table (referenced on the next page)? It's all restored to you in Me, Christ, as you remain immersed in Me, The Trinity, The Community of Believers, The Spirit and Our Word!

The Body-of-Christ	
A.k.a: Body-of-Life, The New Man, The Church, The Redeemed, The Spiritual Man!	
Our state:	Life
Our master/head:	Christ
Our identity:	Sons-of-God
Our reality:	Heavenly/Spiritual (on Earth as it is in Heaven!)
Our language:	Love, Truth & Honor
Our motivation:	The Kingdom of Heaven
Our behavior:	Righteousness (Living in the reality of our blessed Identities) as a result of Love and Truth.
Our code/government:	The Love-Code / Law of the Spirit of Life

Chapter Eighteen

I, Christ

Lecture No 6: I Am The Sabbath

"Sabbath, in the first instance, is not about worship. It is about work stoppage. It is about withdrawal from the anxiety system of Pharaoh, the refusal to let one's life be defined by production and consumption and the endless pursuit of private well-being."

Walter Brueggemann

So! How are you? Keeping up? We've advanced some distance together, and I'm so proud of you. Are you feeling a profound change within? Can you feel the shouts of joy bubbling within your innermost being? Can you hear your song, feel the rhythm of your identity?

In this lecture I want to talk about doing life differently, doing life from a place of security and total rest. So, kick back, relax and enjoy the presentation. We've just about reached our destination!

Salvation Today

Many scriptures encourage you to live in the "today" of your salvation. They come in various forms such as an encouragement to not worry, or an injunction to rejoice in this day. Scripture is making a simple point: focusing your life on anything else but resurrection life today is no life at all. Focusing on yesterday as the reference for tomorrow is resuscitating the Adamic lifestyle. Yesterday will duplicate itself into tomorrow. That lifestyle produces only stress and anxiety. Heaven lives in the I AM of Eternity. There is no yesterday to regret and no tomorrow to worry about. There is simply the NOW of your I AM sustaining every moment. I, Christ, am the reference for your future. I hold the Logos of your "I am" life in Me!

Living in the NOW of our RESURRECTION Life is living in your REST - the Sabbath of today. That's where you enjoy the fullness of salvation. That's where you enjoy Heaven on Earth. That's where the miraculous resides.

Here're a few passages of Scripture to give you a Biblical framework:

"Therefore, while the promise to enter His rest remains, let us fear that none of you should miss it.

For we also have received the good news just as they did; but the message they heard did not benefit them, since they were not united with those who heard it in faith, (for we who have believed enter the rest) (...)

And yet His works have been finished since the foundation of the world, for somewhere He has spoken about the seventh day in this way:

And on the seventh day

God rested from all His works. (...)

Therefore, a Sabbath rest remains for God's people. For the person who has entered His rest has rested from his own works, just as God did from His. Let us then make every effort to enter that rest, so that no one will fall into the same pattern of disobedience."[239]

"Don't fret or worry. Instead of worrying, pray. Let petitions and praises shape your worries into prayers, letting God know your concerns. Before you know it, a sense of God's wholeness, everything coming together for good, will

come and settle you down. It's wonderful what happens when Christ displaces worry at the center of your life." [240]

"This is the day which the LORD has made; Let us rejoice and be glad in it." [241]

"Steep your life in God-reality, God-initiative, God-provisions. Don't worry about missing out. You'll find all your everyday human concerns will be met.

"Give your entire attention to what God is doing right now, and don't get worked up about what may or may not happen tomorrow. God will help you deal with whatever hard things come up when the time comes." [242]

Defining Rest

I know that resting isn't easy, particularly not in Adam's world. But you are not in Adam; you are in Me, Christ. Your focus is on the image of you in Me. I am the Prince of Peace.[243] Remember my words to the disciples? "Do not be troubled[244]"- my Peace I leave with you[245] - I am your Sabbath! As you gaze into the mirror, it is Peace that you see, and you become Peace because I am Peace.

Peace is harmony of the soul. In this place of rest and peace - in Shalom which is sourced in Me your Sabbath - your soul is at rest. It's a profound sense of balance. Living in Sabbath is about living from a place of total well-being and a deep rest in your souls. A soul that knows unconditional love is ruled by peace. Uncontaminated truth empowers you to make wise decisions for tomorrow producing a sense of assurance and peacefulness.

Rest - living in the Sabbath - is freedom from anxiety and disturbance; it's release from worry and insecurity. It means to be inwardly quiet, composed and peaceful. To enter God's rest means to be at peace with God and to possess the perfect peace He gives: *"You will keep him in perfect peace, Whose mind is stayed on You, Because he trusts in You."* [246] Rest encompasses you like a fortress or a force field. When you dwell in a place of rest, your enemies of peace can't produce anxiety, stress, insecurity, worry or fear. You live in a fortress while enjoying life to the full in this earthly realm. You do not escape this world, but you live above its fears, lies and the evil therein.

David describes it this way:

"He who dwells in the shelter of the Most High Will abide in the shadow of the Almighty.

I will say to the LORD, "My refuge and my fortress, My God, in whom I trust!"

For it is He who delivers you from the snare of the trapper And from the deadly pestilence.

He will cover you with His pinions, And under His wings you may seek refuge; His faithfulness is a shield and bulwark.

You will not be afraid of the terror by night, Or of the arrow that flies by day;" [247]

It doesn't mean there aren't battles to fight, but you fight them from a high place of protection. In another Psalm David says:

"I love You, O LORD, my strength."

"The LORD is my rock and my fortress and my deliverer, My God, my rock, in whom I take refuge; My shield and the horn of my salvation, my stronghold."

"I call upon the LORD, who is worthy to be praised, And I am saved from my enemies." [248]

Living in the NOW

It's easy to "relax" in your abilities when you have your act together, and you feel you have a created a secure environment for yourself where everything is under control. But what happens when there is nothing safe in your life except for the promise that God is in control - no house and no job? It is not that easy to enjoy the moment and relax. You start to look for options and solutions. And if you're not careful you are in danger of creating solutions that get you into trouble. Abraham designed a solution to his and Sarah's childlessness. [249] It's a defect of fallen humanity, a character trait that's hard to eradicate. You can't seem to rest until you've created an illusion of comfort and control around you. If you don't, you worry. That mindset is embedded in the Sin-Code, remember?

It's a challenge to accept the NOW you are living in when your mind is anxious about tomorrow. It's impossible! And if you add yesterday's lies, fears and shame, your today feels more like Hell than Heaven. If you want to enjoy rest NOW - because rest is a NOW thing - you need to become totally anxious-free about tomorrow and reconciled to your past. You can't create a comfort zone to produce that kind of peace through self-effort. It doesn't matter how much you try! The more you try, the worse it gets.

Sometimes Abba takes you out of your place of self-made comfort that reveals your anxieties. Then He will put on hold for longer than you can support: nothing seems to be happening not even a glimpse of what the future holds for you. And if He begins to reveal a little, it's never enough. The only thing He seems to say is this: "I am working in your favor - trust me"! You need to learn that rest is found in trusting Us, The Trinity, entirely. If you want to know total peace and rest in this moment, you only need to know one thing: We are working on your behalf, in your favor. Just trust Us!"

You will find rest in total trust.

But more is happening here than meets the eye. When anxieties reveal themselves, it's an opportunity for you to deal with those deep seeded fears that have been out of tune with Heaven's thoughts since who knows when. It's the right moment to let us heal you. It's sometimes very painful, but always very rewarding.

Our promises encompass everything about your life. Abba, Amma and I have it all worked out. Rest is trusting that we are working in your favor even if you can't see or understand how. The Sabbath is resting in us and enjoying the moment. It's being in the I AM! We, Elohim, want you to enjoy every moment knowing that you are where we want you to be each day. Total trust in Us is the foundation of your sense of "being settled and secure." That's where you begin to understand Heaven.

The Children of Israel

The children of Israel had the promise to enter into a place of rest, but they rejected it and missed out. It's not that they wanted to go back into slavery, it's that they had no idea what Our promises were all about because they were still slaves in their hearts. The discomfort of slavery was what they knew, and it felt more normal to them than the Promise Land. Slavery was comfortable to them. They had no reference to understand the land of promise they were heading toward, so they feared it even though it was better for them by a long shot. Often you don't move forward in life because you don't comprehend the promise that is ahead of you. You only understand your past experiences. The effort you place in creating your environments of security and comfort only increase your dependence on slavery. What we, Elohim, were asking Israel to do was to trust Us.

Our promises must be lived to be understood. They can't remain at a level of theory or theology. They must be experienced. But, until you enter into our promises, you need to take Us at our Word. That's why you need to know Us intimately. Rest doesn't come from possessing the promise; rest comes from trusting the One who promised. You can relax NOW if you totally believe Us for your future even if things seem out of control around you. You can remain confident in us and be totally free of worries, even when there's a storm around you. You can even walk on water in the storm. You can trust Us knowing nothing about tomorrow. Rest is found in Me, not in a controlled space you've created for yourself. Peace is enjoying the moment you are in by trusting Us NOW! Enjoying Today. Now is the day of rest!

The Quest Is Over

All this anxiety, fear and control are remnants of the old Adamic lifestyle. The quest is embedded deep in your consciousness. Bad habits die hard. Seek rest. Find peace. You will discover it in Me. You will enter into the Sabbath. Your life will become peace.

And at that moment everything becomes right; all the ingredients come together, a window of opportunity is opened, and you will know, without a doubt that it's time to let go and step out. You will feel the winds blowing in your favor. You will know you have the backing of Heaven. Irresistible forces compel you forward. The time is right. It's not about Kronos time: a date in your diary, time on your clock. No, it's that all things have come together for you. Every moment, every experience, the good and the evil you've encountered, everything has prepared you for this moment. It's not just that; you know that Heaven has destined you, mentored you, guided you and designed you for this. It's Kairos time. Kairos is the appointed time, the moment we, Elohim, have set aside for a particular event when all the elements have come together – crisis time - crunch time: the NOW of our purposes. When you find yourself in the "NOW", the "TODAY" of our purpose you begin to do life differently. You do life from a place of rest, peace, a sense of assignment from within the presence of

God. And you begin to live outwardly from within that position to do Abba's will on Earth as it is in Heaven. It's hard to describe this place, but there's a certainty, a knowing, an assurance, a power within, joy, peace, love and faith. It feels as if your life has come together, and you are stepping into your destiny. It's the Sabbath. (It's not doing nothing but doing everything differently!)

When you find rest, the quest stops. The pursuit of destiny, identity and Sonship ends. The moment you find that position in Me, the instant you enter in, you know! It's the moment you start living from your identity. It's the instant you start fulfilling your destiny. It's when you know that you are Son-of-God. Your life stops being a pursuit. It is now all about living in the eternal NOW of who you are. The hard work ends, and the tending starts. You know who you are. You have found yourself in the I AM. The doing ends, and the being begins. You are you, and you are at peace and in harmony with Heaven and yourself. From that place of being you can do and remain totally rested. You dwell in the Sabbath. That's what I meant when I said, *"The Sabbath was made for man."* [250] We established the Sabbath for you to dwell in and to do life from!

The Sabbath is now, in the I am of Resurrection Life. It is rest for the soul yet in that place all significant things are achieved:

I saved humanity from that place of rest! Moses led the Children of Israel from that place.[251] He wrote the Law in that place of rest. The place of rest is the Ark that Noah built, The Holy of Holies of Moses' Tabernacle.

Hebrews 4 says, *"Therefore, while the promise of entering his rest still stands, (.....) let us (...) strive to enter that rest..."*[252]

Once you have entered, after striving to find it and to enter in, you know it!

It is Kairos time, a place outside of Kronos time inside the NOW of Eternity. You were destined for this. The pursuit is over. You can do life centered in Christ, in peace, in love, in joy, in power. You can do His will. Let it be done on Earth as it is in Heaven.

In the Sabbath you have all you need and know everything you need to know. It's not that you have all the resources. It's certainly not that you know everything. We will never give everything you need from the get go. You need to trust Us. We certainly never reveal everything you need to know. You need to believe Us. It's just that, now, you know Us. You are in Me, and we are in Abba and Amma. You trust! You are at peace in Me. And, you know all of Heaven is working in your favor. It's not wishful thinking. It's not that you're trying to convince yourself. You just know. That knowledge is enough. There are lots of things you don't know. But you know enough! There are resources you don't yet possess on Earth. But you have enough, enough to step into your destiny and to walk by faith always in and from a place of total rest and trust. You are becoming like the one in the Christ-Mirror! Shalom is what I am, and rest is a substance of the Kingdom[253] enjoyed in Me, your Sabbath!

You have found your "I Am!" proclamation.

About the Author

Dave developed an insatiable love for Truth as a teenager, studying Scripture at intensive Bible Camps organized each summer throughout Europe by his church's denomination. He complemented the intensives by attending Bible College in Ontario, Canada. A passionate seeker of God and Truth, Dave believes that the Holy Spirit continues to reveal more to us as we seek to know with openness of heart. A preacher and teacher for close to 30 years now, he has spoken in countries around the globe and served in various ministry roles in France, Australia and overseas as a short-term Missionary with his family. Dave met his future wife Laurence in France where they got married in June 1990. Paris is, after all, the romance capital of the world! They've been living in Australia since 1997. Two boys were added to their lives through the IVF program: Damien in 2002 and Breandan in 2004.

ENDNOTES

---

[1] **Romans 8:14**

[2] **Romans 8:19**

[3] **1 Peter 2:9-10**

--

[4] The Bible suggests that we existed in God's mind before we came into this created realm in physical form with Scriptures such as: **Jeremiah 1:5**, *"Before I formed you in the womb I knew you, And before you were born I consecrated you; I have appointed you a prophet to the nations."*
Psalms 139:14-16, *"I will give thanks to You, for I am fearfully and wonderfully made; Wonderful are Your works, And my soul knows it very well. My frame was not hidden from You, When I was made in secret, And skillfully wrought in the depths of the earth; Your eyes have seen my unformed substance; And in Your book were all written The days that were ordained for me, When as yet there was not one of them."*

--

[5] We will use the term "Cosmos" to describe all things created: the universe including time and space.

--

[6] Author's Comments:

The analogy of family to understand the Trinity is, in my opinion, one of the most powerful and accurate analogies that can be used. The Catholic Church has used this analogy for years so this is not a novel way of explaining the Trinity.

For me, this is not about doctrine or Theology but about relationship. This analogy deepens my relationship with God and is incredibly useful to understand love, affections, submission and many other concepts we'll unveil in this book.

--

[7] **Elohim**

"Elohim" is found 2602 times in the Hebrew Bible (Tanakh, Old Testament). The word is used for: the true God, false gods, supernatural spirits (angels), and human leaders (kings, judges, the Messiah).

The "-im" ending denotes a plural masculine noun. Most of the time, when the noun is used for the true God, it has singular masculine verbs. This is contrary to normal rules of Hebrew grammar. The word "Lord" (Adon) is also often plural (Adonim) with singular verbs.

When used of the true God, "Elohim" denotes what is called by linguists a plural of majesty, honor, or fullness. That is, he is GOD in the fullest sense of the word. He is "GOD of gods" or literally, "ELOHIM of elohim" (Deut 10:17; Ps 136:2). But the Septuagint Greek Bible has "Theos" (a singular noun) for "Elohim." When the NT quotes an OT passage that has "Elohim," the Greek NT uses "Theos," not a plural form.

Paul Sumner, "'Elohim' in Biblical Context" [http://www.hebrew-streams.org/works/monotheism/context-elohim.html. Accessed 8-26-15].

--

[8] **Yahweh or Jehovah**

The special and significant name (not merely an appellative title such as Lord [adonai]) by which God revealed himself to the ancient Hebrews (Exodus 6:2 Exodus 6:3). This name, the Tetragrammaton of the Greeks, was held by the later Jews to be so sacred that it was never pronounced except by the high priest on the great Day of Atonement, when he entered into the most holy place. Whenever this name occurred in the sacred books they pronounced it, as they still do, "Adonai" (i.e., Lord), thus using another word in its stead. The Massorets gave to it the vowel-points appropriate to this word. This Jewish practice was founded on a false interpretation of Leviticus 24:16 . The meaning of the word appears from Exodus 3:14 to be "the unchanging, eternal, self-existent God," the "I am that I am," a convenant-keeping God. (Compare Malachi 3:6 ; Hosea 12:5 ; Revelation 1:4 Revelation 1:8 .)

Taken from M.G. Easton M.A., D.D., Illustrated Bible Dictionary, Third Edition, published by Thomas Nelson, 1897. Public Domain, copy freely.

--

[9] **Genesis 1:1**

[10] **John 1:1**

[11] **1 John 4:18**

[12] **Genesis 1:3**

[13] **Romans 1:20**

--

[14] **Colossians 1:16** , *“For by Him all things were created, [both] in the heavens and on earth, visible and invisible, whether thrones or dominions or rulers or authorities-- all things have been created through Him and for Him.”*

[15] **Genesis 1:10, 12, 18, 21, 25**

[16] **Genesis 1:26-27**

26 Then God said, "Let Us make man in Our image, according to Our likeness; and let them rule over the fish of the sea and over the birds of the sky and over the cattle and over all the earth, and over every creeping thing that creeps on the earth." 27 “God created man in His own image, in the image of God He created him; male and female He created them.”

--

[17] **Colossians 1:16-17**
[18] **Ephesians 1:4-6**

--
[19] **Mark 1:9-11**
9 "In those days Jesus came from Nazareth in Galilee and was baptized by John in the Jordan. 10 Immediately coming up out of the water, He saw the heavens opening, and the Spirit like a dove descending upon Him; 11 and a voice came out of the heavens: 'You are My beloved Son, in You I am well-pleased.' "
---

[20] This idea is developed in the chapter entitled "I, Adam, Am Immature"
--
[21] **Psalm 8:3-8, 3,** *"When I consider Your heavens, the work of Your fingers, The moon and the stars, which You have ordained;4What is man that You take thought of him, And the son of man that You care for him?5Yet You have made him a little lower than God, And You crown him with glory and majesty! 6You make him to rule over the works of Your hands; You have put all things under his feet,7All sheep and oxen, And also the beasts of the field, 8The birds of the heavens and the fish of the sea, Whatever passes through the paths of the seas."*
--

[22] **Genesis 2:18-20, 18,** *"Then the LORD God said, 'It is not good for the man to be alone; I will make him a helper suitable for him.' 19Out of the ground the LORD God formed every beast of the field and every bird of the sky, and brought [them] to the man to see what he would call them; and whatever the man called a living creature, that was its name." 20The man gave names to all the cattle, and to the birds of the sky, and to every beast of the field, but for Adam there was not found a helper suitable for him."*
--

[23] **Genesis 2:7,** *"Then the LORD God formed man of dust from the ground, and breathed into his nostrils the breath of life; and man became a living being."*
--

---

[24] **Ecclesiastes 3:11**, *"He has made everything appropriate in its time. He has also set eternity in their heart, yet so that man will not find out the work which God has done from the beginning even to the end."*

--

[25] **Acts 17:28**

[26] **1 John 4:13**

--

[27] **Psalm 8, 3,** *"When I look at the night sky and see the work of your fingers-- the moon and the stars you set in place--4 what are mere mortals that you should think about them, human beings that you should care for them? 5 Yet you made them only a little lower than God and crowned them[e] with glory and honor. 6 You gave them charge of everything you made, putting all things under their authority--7 the flocks and the herds and all the wild animals, 8 the birds in the sky, the fish in the sea, and everything that swims the ocean currents."*

--

[28] **Genesis 2:25**

[29] **Genesis 2:18-25, 18,** *"Then the LORD God said, "It is not good for the man to be alone; I will make him a helper suitable for him." 19 Out of the ground the LORD God formed every beast of the field and every bird of the sky, and brought [them] to the man to see what he would call them; and whatever the man called a living creature, that was its name. 20The man gave names to all the cattle, and to the birds of the sky, and to every beast of the field, but for Adam there was not found a helper suitable for him. 21So the LORD God caused a deep sleep to fall upon the man, and he slept; then He took one of his ribs and closed up the flesh at that place. 22The LORD God fashioned into a woman the rib which He had taken from the man, and brought her to the man. 23The man said, 'This is now bone of my bones, And flesh of my flesh; She shall be called Woman, Because she was taken out of Man.' 24For this reason a man shall leave his father and his mother, and be joined to his wife; and they shall become one flesh. 25And the man and his wife were both naked and were not ashamed."*

--

[30] **Genesis 2:23-24**

[31] **Psalm 8:3-8 (see text above)**

---

32 **1 John 4:16,** "We have come to know and have believed the love which God has for us. God is love, and the one who abides in love abides in God, and God abides in him."

---

33 In a fallen world desires are turned to lust and affections towards materialistic things instead of finding fulfillment in relationships.

---

34 **James 1:18**

35 **Genesis 1:26**

--

36 Jesus confirms this when He says, *"I am the door; if anyone enters through Me, he will be saved, and will go in and out and find pasture."* - John 10:9

Other Scriptures confirm this notion:

John 14:6, *"I am the way and the truth and the life. No one comes to the Father except through me."*

Ephesians 2:18, *"For through him we both have access by one Spirit to the Father."*

--

37 The author of Hebrews writes this: *"He (God) disciplines us for our good, so that we may share His holiness"*□ . **Hebrews 12:10.** In the context of this passage the author is talking about our Sonship in regards to our relationship with God. Just prior to this statement he says: *"God deals with you as with sons ; for what son is there whom his father does not discipline?"* **Hebrews 12:7b**□. Sonship and holiness work hand in hand.

--

38 **Ephesians 4:24**

--

39 In **Revelations 13 verse 8**, the Kings James Version of the Bible mentions "the Lamb slain from the foundation of the world." This idea will be expanded in the following paragraphs.

--

40 Author's testimony:

I was raised in an environment that encouraged the pursuit of holiness as a personal effort to evict sin from our lives. We called it "sanctification." "Sanctification," according to the Bible, is the act of setting a person or thing aside for a specific purpose. One cannot sanctify oneself. God sanctified the Levites for service. It is impossible to be holy (as in sanctified) unless an outside authority sanctifies you. We were wrongly taught to pursue self-sanctification. That environment produced a belief system that one could become Holy through compliance with standards and personal works. The standard became Law. The reality was that total compliance proved impossible and led to many problems. We strived to "keep up the appearance of holiness." We became judgmental and critical of those who did not conform. We lived in guilt and condemnation at the realization that the eradication of our secret "sinful behaviors" had proved impossible.

--

[41] In God's Kingdom, Rulership is expressed with the heart of Fathers. God said to Adam and Eve, *"... rule over the fish of the sea and over the birds of the sky and over every living thing that moves on the earth"* Genesis 1:28.

--

[42] **Revelation 13:8 (KJV)**, *"And all that dwell upon the earth shall worship him (the beast), whose names are not written in the book of life of the Lamb slain from the foundation of the world."*
A study of this topic (Book of Life) reveals that names of sinners will be blotted out of the Book-of-Life."

Revelation 3:5 (KJV)

"He that overcometh, the same shall be clothed in white raiment; and I will not blot out his name out of the book of life, but I will confess his name before my Father, and before his angels."

These passages suggest that every name was in the Book to start with. Further along in this book we will see that Adam was "The Sinner" and all have been given the right to escape his Deadness. I believe all will have the opportunity to accept or reject the offering of Resurrection Life in Christ but first the free moral agency of each must be restored. In other words this is not a choice one can make without a healing and cleansing of the heart and soul.

[43] Sacramentalisation / Sacramental Act:

A sacrament is a religious ceremony that confirms a spiritual reality. Protestant churches have retained 2 sacraments: baptism and communion. The Catholic Church has 7: baptism, penance, confirmation, the Eucharist, holy orders, matrimony, and the anointing of the sick. In my opinion ordination (holy orders), the anointing of the sick and matrimony (marriage) should be considered as sacraments as a ceremony on Earth that reflects a reality that has occurred or been ordained in Heaven.

Jesus' crucifixion, burial and resurrection on Earth was a sacramental act that confirmed on Earth what had already taken place before time.

Revelation 13:8 (KJV)
"And all that dwell upon the earth shall worship him, whose names are not written in the book of life of the Lamb slain from the foundation of the world."
1 Peter 1:20 (GW)
"He is the lamb who was known long ago before the world existed, but for your good he became publicly known in the last period of time."
--

[44] **Psalms 139:5 (NLT)**

[45] **Psalms 139:16-17 (NLT)**

[46] **1John 4:8**

[47] **1John 4:7-9**
"Beloved, let us love one another, for love is from God; and everyone who loves is born of God and knows God. 8 The one who does not love does not know God, for God is love. 9 By this the love of God was manifested in us, that God has sent His only begotten Son into the world so that we might live through Him."
--

[48] **Genesis 3:8**
"They heard the sound of the LORD God walking in the garden in the cool of the day." Although this verse takes place after the Fall; the inference is that Adam, Eve and God did this on an ongoing basis.
--

[49] **1John 4:16**

[50] **1Corinthians 13:12-13**

[51] **Genesis 1:28**

[52] **John 1:14**

[53] **Hebrews 6:18**

[54] **John 8:32**

[55] **Colossians 3:12-17**

[56] **Colossians 3:15**

[57] **Philippians 4:7**

[58] **Colossians 3:16**

[59] **Proverbs 9:10**

[60] **Proverbs 9:16**

[61] **Proverbs 21:19**

[62] **Colossians 3:12-17**

[63] **Proverbs 21:19**

[64] **3 John 1:2**

--

[65] See Chapter 5: **I, Adam, Am Immature**

--

[66] Paul refers to the two Adam's in two instances. In his Epistle to the Romans and to the Corinthians. The two Adams will be unpacked throughout this book.
Romans 5:12-21, 1 Corinthians 15:20-23

--

[67] **Hebrews 5:8**

"Although He was a Son, He learned obedience from the things which He suffered."

--

[68] **Hebrews 5:9 (HCSB)**

"After He was perfected, He became the source of eternal salvation for all who obey Him,..."

--

[69] **Hebrews 5:8-9**

[70] **John 10:18**

[71] **Genesis 2:16-17**

--

[72] Pronoia (pro-nous) means before-mind: the mind or thinking you have before the exercise of your will. See footnote below re: metanoia.

--

[73] **Colossians 3:2-3**

2 "Set your mind on the things above, not on the things that are on earth.
3 For you have died and your life is hidden with Christ in God."

--

[74] **Colossians 3:4**

4 "When Christ, who is our life, is revealed, then you also will be revealed with Him in glory."

[75] Metanoia

Metanoia is a word filled with remarkable meaning by the preaching of Christ and the apostles. It is not a word that comes replete with it's own meaning. The English word "repentance," on the other hand, comes filled with it's own meaning - it needs no supplementing by context. Repentance means to feel remorse or regret for your sins; it's Latin root literally means "pain; suffering in view of being liable to punishment." Metanoia has no such meaning associated with it. The word is Greek, and it is made up of two words: meta & nous. Meta means "after" or "change," and nous is the Greek word for "mind." The word means "after-mind" and signifies a change of mind: thinking one way, but then afterwards thinking another. It is the opposite of pronoia (pro-nous) which means before-mind: the mind or thinking you have before. Interestingly, there is another Greek word we frequently use in English that is related to metanoia: it is paranoia (para-nous). Literally, the word means to be beside-mind, or we would say "out of your mind," or "beside yourself." Paranoia is not being in a right mind, but having a mind that is off center - that is, not where it should be. (http://www.etymonline.com/index.php?term=paranoia&allowed_in_frame=0). If you compare metanoia and paranoia together, you get the idea of what the New Testament calls for metanoia is: it is a command to change your mind and get it where it should be.

Eli Brayley, "The Great Meaning of Metanoia" [http://www.timothyministry.com/2012/07/the-great-meaning-of-metanoia.html accessed 8-27-15]

The best translation for metanoia is "mind-shift" or "change-of-mind."

--

[76] **Genesis 2:16b-17**

[77] **James 1:2-4**

[78] **Genesis 3:1-5**

1 "Now the serpent was more crafty than any beast of the field which the LORD God had made. And he said to the woman, "Indeed, has God said, 'You shall not eat from any tree of the garden?" 2 The woman said to the serpent, 'From the fruit of the trees of the garden we may eat; 3 but from the fruit of the tree which is in the middle of the garden, God has said, 'You shall not eat from it or touch it, or you will die.' 4 The serpent said to the woman, 'You surely will not die! 5 For God knows that in the day you eat from it your eyes will be opened, and you will be like God, knowing good and evil.' "

[79] **Genesis 3:5**

[80] **Proverbs 9:10**

[81] **John 8:44**

---

[82] **Romans 6:16**
[83] **Romans 1:20-25**

--
[84] James 3
16 "For where jealousy and selfish ambition exist, there is disorder and every evil thing. 17 But the wisdom from above is first pure, then peaceable, gentle, reasonable, full of mercy and good fruits, unwavering, without hypocrisy. 18 And the seed whose fruit is righteousness is sown in peace by those who make peace."

--

[85] **Psalm 116:11**

--
[86] **John 18:37**
"...for this reason I was born, and for this I came into the world, to testify to the truth. Everyone on the side of truth listens to me."

John 5:24 *"I tell you the truth, ...*

John 14:5 *"Thomas said to Him, 'Lord, we do not know where You are going, how do we know the way?' 6 Jesus said to him, "I am the way, and the truth, and the life; no one comes to the Father but through Me. 7 If you had known Me, you would have known My Father also; from now on you know Him, and have seen Him. . ."*

--

[87] **Revelation 21:8**
"But for the cowardly and unbelieving and abominable and murderers and immoral persons and sorcerers and idolaters and all liars, their part will be in the lake that burns with fire and brimstone, which is the second death."

--
[88] **Genesis 3:7**
[89] **Job 18:5-6**
[90] **Romans 3:23**
[91] **Hebrews 11:1a**
[92] **1 Corinthians 4:4**
[93] **Genesis 6:5**
[94] **Genesis 3:8-10**
[95] **Psalm 3:3-6**
[96] **Genesis 3:5**

---

[97] **Job 3:25**
[98] **1John 4:18b**

[99] **John 5:22**
"For not even the Father judges anyone, but He has given all judgment to the Son,.."

[100] **John 8:15-17**
"You judge according to the flesh; I am not judging anyone. 16 "But even if I do judge, My judgment is true; for I am not alone in it, but I and the Father who sent Me. 17"Even in your law it has been written that the testimony of two men is true. . ."
--

[101] **Psalms 23:4**
[102] **Genesis 3:8-10**
[103] **Genesis 3:8-10**

[104] **Hebrews 2:14-16**
". . . 14 Therefore, since the children share in flesh and blood, He Himself likewise also partook of the same, that through death He might render powerless him who had the power of death, that is, the devil, 15 and might free those who through fear of death were subject to slavery all their lives. 16 For assuredly He does not give help to angels, but He gives help to the descendant of Abraham. . . "

[105] **John 3:19**
"This is the judgment, that the Light has come into the world, and men loved the darkness rather than the Light, for their deeds were evil. 20 For everyone who does evil hates the Light, and does not come to the Light for fear that his deeds will be exposed. 21 "But he who practices the truth comes to the Light, so that his deeds may be manifested as having been wrought in God."
--

[106] **Genesis 3:14-19**
14 "So the Lord God said to the serpent, 'Because you have done this, cursed are you above all livestock and all wild animals! You will crawl on your belly and you will eat dust all the days of your life. 15 And I will put enmity between you and the woman, and between your offspring and hers; he will crush your head, and you will strike his heel. 16 To the woman he said, 'I will make your pains in childbearing very severe; with

---

painful labor you will give birth to children. Your desire will be for your husband, and he will rule over you.' 17 To Adam he said, 'Because you listened to your wife and ate fruit from the tree about which I commanded you, 'You must not eat from it,' Cursed is the ground because of you; through painful toil you will eat food from it all the days of your life. 18 It will produce thorns and thistles for you, and you will eat the plants of the field. 19 By the sweat of your brow you will eat your food until you return to the ground, since from it you were taken; for dust you are and to dust you will return."

--

[107] **Mark 7:14-16**

[108] **Mark 7:18-23**

[109] **Genesis 6:5**

--

[110] This is what Paul is referring to in **Romans 12:2** when he says do not be conformed to this world (present age - Cosmos), but be transformed by the renewing of your mind, so that you may prove what the will of God is, that which is good and acceptable and perfect.

--

[111] **Isaiah 55:1-2**, *"Ho! Every one who thirsts, come to the waters; And you who have no money come, buy and eat. Come, buy wine and milk without money and without cost. 2 "Why do you spend money for what is not bread, And your wages for what does not satisfy? Listen carefully to Me, and eat what is good, And delight yourself in abundance. . . "*

Matthew 5:6 , *"Blessed are those who hunger and thirst for righteousness, for they will be filled."*

John 4:14, *"But whoever drinks the water I give them will never thirst. Indeed, the water I give them will become in them a spring of water welling up to eternal life."*

[112] **John 7:37-38**

[113] **Galatians 5:19-21 (NET)**

--

[114] **1 Corinthians 15:22**

"For as in Adam all die, so also in Christ all will be made alive."

--

[115] **Luke 4:5-7**

"And he led Him up and showed Him all the kingdoms of the world in a moment of time. 6 And the devil said to Him, 'I will give You all this domain and its glory; for it has been handed over to me, and I give it to whomever I wish. 7 Therefore if You worship before me, it shall all be Yours.'"

---

[116] **Matthew 28:18-20**
"And Jesus came up and spoke to them, saying, 'All authority has been given to Me in heaven and on earth. 19"Go therefore and make disciples of all the nations, baptizing them in the name of the Father and the Son and the Holy Spirit, 20 teaching them to observe all that I commanded you; and lo, I am with you always, even to the end of the age."'

--

[117] **John 8:44**

[118] **Matthew 10:24-25**

[119] **Colossians 2:10-12**
"And in Him you have been made complete, and He is the head over all rule and authority; 11and in Him you were also circumcised with a circumcision made without hands, in the removal of the body of the flesh by the circumcision of Christ; 12 having been buried with Him in baptism, in which you were also raised up with Him through faith in the working of God, who raised Him from the dead . . ."

[120] **Romans 6:6**
"For we know that our old self was crucified with him so that the body ruled by sin might be done away with, that we should no longer be slaves to sin . . ."

[121] **Romans 7:24**
"Wretched man that I am! Who will set me free from the body of this death?"

--

[122] **Ephesians 2:1-3**

--

[123] Richard J. Foster, *Celebration of Discipline: The Path to Spiritual Growth*

--

[124] **Romans 7:12 (NAS)**

--

[125] **Romans 7:8-13 (NLT)**
"but sin took advantage of this law and aroused all kinds of forbidden desires within me! If there were no law, sin would not have that power. I felt fine when I did not understand what the law demanded. But when I learned the truth, I realized I had broken the law and was a sinner, doomed to die. So the good law, which was supposed to show me the way of life, instead gave me the death penalty. Sin took advantage of the law and fooled me; it took the good law and used it to make me guilty of death. But still, the law itself is holy and right and good. But how can that be? Did the law, which is good, cause my doom? Of course not! Sin used what was good to bring about my condemnation. So we can see

how terrible sin really is. It uses God's good commandment for its own evil purposes."

--

[126] **Romans 7:18-24**

--

[127] See the movie "I Robot" which is an adaptation of Isaac Asimov's novels.

--

[128] **Romans 7:1-2 (NKJ)**

[129] **Genesis 2:16-17**

[130] **Romans 5:12-14 (The Mirror Bible)**

--

[131] **Genesis 5:3-5**

"When Adam had lived one hundred and thirty years, he became the father of a son in his own likeness, according to his image, and named him Seth. 4 Then the days of Adam after he became the father of Seth were eight hundred years, and he had other sons and daughters. 5 So all the days that Adam lived were nine hundred and thirty years, and he died. . . "

--

[132] Genesis 2:17 says, *"In the day that you eat from it you will surely die." In God's eyes one day is like a thousand years.* **2 Peter 3:8** *says, "But do not let this one fact escape your notice, beloved, that with the Lord one day is like a thousand years, and a thousand years like one day."*

--

[133] **1John 4:2**

"By this you know the Spirit of God: every spirit that confesses that Jesus Christ has come in the flesh is from God."

John 1:14, *"The Word became flesh and made his dwelling among us. We have seen his glory, the glory of the one and only Son, who came from the Father, full of grace and truth."*

[134] **Philippians 2:5-8**

"Have this attitude in yourselves which was also in Christ Jesus, 6who, although He existed in the form of God, did not_regard equality with God a thing to be grasped, 7but emptied Himself, taking the form of a bond-servant, and being made in the likeness of men. 8 Being found in appearance as a man, He humbled Himself by becoming obedient to the point of death, even death on a cross."

--

---

[135] **Hebrews 2:17-18**
"Therefore, He had to be made like His brethren in all things, so that He might become a merciful and faithful high priest in things pertaining to God, to make propitiation for the sins of the people. 18For since He Himself was tempted in that which He has suffered, He is able to come to the aid of those who are tempted."

--

[136] **Romans 5:12**

[137] **1Corinthians 15:45-48**
"So also it is written, 'The first man, Adam, became a living soul.' The last Adam became a life-giving spirit. 46 However, the spiritual is not first, but the natural; then the spiritual. 47 The first man is from the earth, [a]earthy; the second man is from heaven. 48 As is the earthy, so also are those who are earthy; and as is the heavenly, so also are those who are heavenly."

--

[138] **2 Corinthians 5:21**
"He made Him who knew no sin to be sin on our behalf, so that we might become the righteousness of God in Him."

--

[139] The genealogy of Jesus according to Luke traces Jesus' lineage right back to Adam. Luke 3:23-38

--

[140] **Matthew 27:45-46**
45 "Now from the sixth hour darkness fell upon all the land until the ninth hour. 46About the ninth hour Jesus cried out with a loud voice, saying, 'ELI, ELI, LAMA SABACHTHANI?' that is, 'MY GOD, MY GOD, WHY HAVE YOU FORSAKEN ME?' "

The orphan spirit has a sense of alienation from their Fathers with this unanswerable question: Why did you forsake me / leave me?

--

[141] **1 Peter 2:24**
"And He Himself bore our sins in His body on the cross, so that we might die to sin and live to righteousness; for by His wounds you were healed."

--

[142] **Romans 5:12-13**
"Therefore, just as through one man sin entered into the world, and death through sin, and so death spread to all men, because all sinned--

13for until the Law sin was in the world, but sin is not imputed when there is no law...."

--
[143] **Romans 5:20-21**
"The Law came in so that the transgression would increase; but where sin increased, grace abounded all the more, 21 so that, as sin reigned in death, even so grace would reign through righteousness to eternal life through Jesus Christ our Lord."

--
[144] **Hebrews 2:14-15 (NLT)**

--
[145] **Colossians 2:13-14**
"When you were dead in your transgressions and the uncircumcision of your flesh, He made you alive together with Him, having forgiven us all our transgressions, 14 having canceled out the certificate of debt consisting of decrees against us, which was hostile to us; and He has taken it out of the way, having nailed it to the cross."

--
[146] **Romans 7:23-25**

--
[147] **Romans 7:1-4**
"...do you not know, brethren (for I speak to those who know the law), that the law has dominion over a man as long as he lives? For the woman who has a husband is bound by the law to her husband as long as he lives. But if the husband dies, she is released from the law of her husband. So then if, while her husband lives, she marries another man, she will be called an adulteress; but if her husband dies, she is free from that law, so that she is no adulteress, though she has married another man. Therefore, my brethren, you also have become dead to the law through the body of Christ, that you may be married to another..."

--
[148] **Hebrews 2:15**

--
[149] **John 1:14**
"And the Word became flesh, and dwelt among us, and we saw His glory, glory as of the only begotten from the Father, full of grace and truth."

--
[150] **John 1:1-5**
"1 In the beginning was the Word, and the Word was with God, and the Word was God. 2 He was in the beginning with God. 3 All things came into being through Him, and apart from Him nothing came into being that

has come into being. 4 In Him was life, and the life was the Light of men. 5 The Light shines in the darkness, and the darkness did not comprehend it."

--

[151] **1 Peter 3:18-20**

"For Christ also died for sins once for all, the just for the unjust, so that He might bring us to God, having been put to death in the flesh, but made alive in the spirit; 19 in which also He went and made proclamation to the spirits now in prison, 20 who once were disobedient, when the patience of God kept waiting in the days of Noah, during the construction of the ark, in which a few, that is, eight persons, were brought safely through the water."

--

[152] Jesus died on Thursday night and rose on Sunday morning. He rose "on the third day" but actually spent a little over 2 days in the grave. (2 days represent 2000 years and a bit.)

--

[153] **Revelation 3:5**

"He who overcomes will thus be clothed in white garments; and I will not erase his name from the book of life, and I will confess his name before My Father and before His angels."

--

[154] **Luke 15:11-32**

"11 And He said, 'A man had two sons. 12 The younger of them said to his father,' 'Father, give me the share of the estate that falls to me.' So he divided his wealth between them. 13 And not many days later, the younger son gathered everything together and went on a journey into a distant country, and there he squandered his estate with loose living. 14 Now when he had spent everything, a severe famine occurred in that country, and he began to be impoverished. 15 So he went and hired himself out to one of the citizens of that country, and he sent him into his fields to feed swine. 16 And he would have gladly filled his stomach with the pods that the swine were eating, and no one was giving [anything] to him. 17 But when he came to his senses, he said, 'How many of my father's hired men have more than enough bread, but I am dying here with hunger! 18 I will get up and go to my father, and will say to him, 'Father, I have sinned against heaven, and in your sight; 19 I am no longer worthy to be called your son; make me as one of your hired men.' 20 So he got up and came to his father. But while he was still a long way off, his father saw him and felt compassion [for him], and ran and embraced him and kissed him. 21 And the son said to him, 'Father, I have sinned against heaven and in your sight; I am no longer worthy to be called your son.' 22 But the father said to his slaves, 'Quickly bring out

the best robe and put it on him, and put a ring on his hand and sandals on his feet; 23 and bring the fattened calf, kill it, and let us eat and celebrate; 24 for this son of mine was dead and has come to life again; he was lost and has been found.' And they began to celebrate.
25 Now his older son was in the field, and when he came and approached the house, he heard music and dancing. 26 And he summoned one of the servants and [began] inquiring what these things could be. 27 And he said to him, 'Your brother has come, and your father has killed the fattened calf because he has received him back safe and sound.' 28 But he became angry and was not willing to go in; and his father came out and [began] pleading with him. 29 But he answered and said to his father, 'Look! For so many years I have been serving you and I have never neglected a command of yours; and [yet] you have never given me a young goat, so that I might celebrate with my friends; 30 but when this son of yours came, who has devoured your wealth with prostitutes, you killed the fattened calf for him.' 31 And he said to him, 'Son, you have always been with me, and all that is mine is yours. 32 But we had to celebrate and rejoice, for this brother of yours was dead and [has begun] to live, and [was] lost and has been found.' "

--

[155] **1 Peter 3:18**

--

[156] **John 1:1-14**

"1 In the beginning was the Word, and the Word was with God, and the Word was God. 2 He was in the beginning with God. 3 All things came into being through Him, and apart from Him nothing came into being that has come into being. (...) 14 And the Word became flesh, and dwelt among us, and we saw His glory, glory as of the only begotten from the Father, full of grace and truth."

--

[157] The Holy Spirit conceived Jesus in Mary's womb:

Luke 1:26-38 " *26 In the sixth month of Elizabeth's pregnancy, God sent the angel Gabriel to Nazareth, a town in Galilee, 27 to a virgin pledged to be married to a man named Joseph, a descendant of David. The virgin's name was Mary. 28 The angel went to her and said, 'Greetings, you who are highly favored! The Lord is with you.' 29 Mary was greatly troubled at his words and wondered what kind of greeting this might be. 30 But the angel said to her, 'Do not be afraid, Mary; you have found favor with God. 31 You will conceive and give birth to a son, and you are to call him Jesus. 32 He will be great and will be called the Son of the Most High. The Lord God will give him the throne of his father David, 33 and he will reign over Jacob's descendants forever; his kingdom will never end.'"34 'How will this be,' Mary asked the angel, 'since I am a virgin?' 35 The angel answered, 'The Holy Spirit will come on you, and the power of the Most High will overshadow you. So the_holy one to be born will be called the Son of God. 36 Even Elizabeth your relative is going to have a child in her old age, and she who was said to be unable to conceive is in her sixth month. 37 For no word from God will ever fail.' 38 'I am the Lord's servant," Mary answered. 'May your word to me be fulfilled.' Then the angel left her."*

John 1:14

"And the Word became flesh, and dwelt among us, and we saw His glory, glory as of the only begotten from the Father, full of grace and truth."
John 3:16
"For God so loved the world, that He gave His only begotten Son, that whoever believes in Him shall not perish, but have eternal life."
--

[158] **Isaiah 7:14**
"Therefore the Lord himself will give you a sign: The virgin will conceive and give birth to a son, and will call him Immanuel."
Matthew 1:22-23
"Now all this took place to fulfill what was spoken by the Lord through the prophet: 23 'BEHOLD, THE VIRGIN SHALL BE WITH CHILD AND SHALL BEAR A SON, AND THEY SHALL CALL HIS NAME IMMANUEL,' which translated means, 'GOD WITH US.' "
--
[159] **1 Corinthians 15:45-49**
[160] **1 Corinthians 15:19-22**
[161] Colossians 1:18
[162] **Revelations 1:5**
[163] **John 11:21**
[164] **John 11:25-26**
[165] **Revelation 1:18**
[166] **Romans 6:9 (KJV)**
[167] **Ephesians 5:23**
"Christ is the head of the church, his body, of which he is the Savior."
Colossians 1:18, *"And he is the head of the body, the church!"*

[168] **Romans 5:14-18**
14 "Nevertheless death reigned from Adam until Moses, even over those who had not sinned in the likeness of the offense of Adam, who is a type

of Him who was to come.15 But the free gift is not like the transgression. For if by the transgression of the one the many died, much more did the grace of God and the gift by the grace of the one Man, Jesus Christ, abound to the many. 16 The gift is not like [that which came] through the one who sinned; for on the one hand the judgment [arose] from one [transgression] resulting in condemnation, but on the other hand the free gift [arose] from many transgressions resulting in justification. 17 For if by the transgression of the one, death reigned through the one, much more those who receive the abundance of grace and of the gift of righteousness will reign in life through the One, Jesus Christ.18 So then as through one transgression there resulted condemnation to all men, even so through one act of righteousness there resulted justification of life to all men."

[169] **Matthew 16:13-20**

"When Jesus came to the region of Caesarea Philippi, he asked his disciples, 'Who do people say the Son of Man is?' They replied, 'Some say

Matthew 16:13-20 Cont'd. – John the Baptist; others say Elijah; and still others, Jeremiah or one of the prophets.' 'But what about you?' he asked. 'Who do you say I am?' Simon Peter answered, 'You are the Messiah, the Son of the living God.' Jesus replied, 'Blessed are you, Simon son of Jonah, for this was not revealed to you by flesh and blood, but by my Father in heaven. And I tell you that you are Peter, and on this rock I will build my church, and the gates of Hades will not overcome it. I will give you the keys of the kingdom of heaven; whatever you bind on earth will be bound in heaven, and whatever you loose on earth will be loosed in heaven. Then he ordered his disciples not to tell anyone that he was the Messiah."

--

[170] **Philippians 2:6-7**

[171] **Romans 1:3-4**

"...concerning His Son, who was born of a descendant of David according to the flesh, who was declared the Son of God with power by the resurrection from the dead, according to the Spirit of holiness, Jesus Christ our Lord,..."

[172] **Romans 1:3-4**

". . . concerning His Son, who was born of a descendant of David according to the flesh, who was declared the Son of God with power by the resurrection from the dead, according to the Spirit of holiness, Jesus Christ our Lord,..."

--

[173] **Matthew 28:18**

--

---

[174] Read the full story in Acts chapter 2.

--

[175] **1 Corinthians 12:12-13**

"12 For even as the body is one and yet has many members, and all the members of the body, though they are many, are one body, so also is Christ. 13 For by one Spirit we were all baptized into one body, whether Jews or Greeks, whether slaves or free, and we were all made to drink of one Spirit."

--

[176] **Galatians 3:26-29**

"26 For you are all sons of God through faith in Christ Jesus. 27 For all of you who were baptized into Christ have clothed yourselves with Christ. 28 There is neither Jew nor Greek, there is neither slave nor free man, there is neither male nor female; for you are all one in Christ Jesus. 29 And if you belong to Christ, then you are Abraham's descendants, heirs according to promise."

--

[177] Anti meaning "in stead of"

--

[178] **John 2:19 -**

in Mark this reference is used to accuse Jesus:

Mark 14:58

"We heard Him say, 'I will destroy this temple made with hands, and in three days I will build another made without hands.'"

--

[179] **John 2:21-22**

--

[180] The Apostle Paul adds to the Temple analogy in his teachings.

To the church in Corinth he says: *"You are ... God's building. According to the grace of God which was given to me, like a wise master builder I laid a foundation, and another is building on it. But each man must be careful how he builds on it. For no man can lay a foundation other than the one which is laid, which is Jesus Christ....Do you not know that you are a temple of God?"*

1 Corinthians 3:9b-16a

To the Colossians he uses the same ideas and adds: *". . .having been built on the foundation of the apostles and prophets, Christ Jesus*

Himself being the corner stone, in whom the whole building, being fitted together, is growing into a holy temple in the Lord, in whom you also are being built together into a dwelling of God in the Spirit. "Ephesians 2:20-22

--

[181] **Romans 8:1-3**
[182] **Hebrews 8:10**
[183] **John 13:34-35**
[184] **Romans 1:16-17**
[185] **Romans 6:23**
[186] **1 John 4:15**
[187] **Colossians 3:3**
[188] **Romans 6:11**
[189] **Romans 8:9**
[190] **Romans 6:4-11**
[191] **Galatians 3:26-27**
[192] **Colossians 3:2-4**
[193] **Colossians 2:9-11**
[194] **2 Corinthians 5:21**
[195] **Romans 8:1**
[196] **Ephesians 1:4-5**
[197] **2 Corinthians 5:17**
[198] **John 11:25**
[199] **Ephesians 2:14-15 (NKJ)**
[200] **1 John 4:18**
[201] **Colossians 2:20**
[202] **John 3:1-15**

1"Now there was a man of the Pharisees, named Nicodemus, a ruler of the Jews; 2this man came to Jesus by night and said to Him, "Rabbi, we know that You have come from God [as] a teacher; for no one can do these signs that You do unless God is with him." 3Jesus answered and said to him,_"Truly, truly, I say to you, unless one is born again he cannot see the kingdom of God."4Nicodemus said to Him, "How can a man be born when he is old? He cannot enter a second time into his mother's womb and be born, can he?" 5Jesus answered, "Truly, truly, I say to you, unless one is born of water and the Spirit he cannot enter into the kingdom of God. 6"That which is born of the flesh is flesh, and that which is born of the Spirit is spirit. 7"Do not be amazed that I said to you, 'You must be born again.' 8"The wind blows where it wishes and you hear the

sound of it, but do not know where it comes from and where it is going; so is everyone who is born of the Spirit."
9Nicodemus said to Him, "How can these things be?" 10Jesus answered and said to him, "Are you the teacher of Israel and do not understand these things? 11"Truly, truly, I say to you, we speak of what we know and testify of what we have seen, and you do not accept our testimony. 12"If I told you earthly things and you do not believe, how will you believe if I tell you heavenly things? 13"No one has ascended into heaven, but He who descended from heaven: the Son of Man. 14"As Moses lifted up the serpent in the wilderness, even so must the Son of Man be lifted up; 15so that whoever believes will in Him have eternal life."

--
[203] **Romans 14:17**

"For the kingdom of God is not eating and drinking, but righteousness and peace and joy in the Holy Spirit.

--
[204] **Acts 14**

"21 After they had preached the gospel to that city and had made many disciples, they returned to Lystra and to Iconium and to Antioch, 22 strengthening the souls of the disciples, encouraging them to continue in the faith, and [saying], "Through many tribulations we must enter the kingdom of God."

--

[205] **Romans 8**

"28 And we know that God causes all things to work together for good to those who love God, to those who are called according to [His] purpose."

--
[206] **2 Corinthians 5:17**

--
[207] **Hebrews 12:1-2**

"Therefore, since we have so great a cloud of witnesses surrounding us, let us also lay aside every encumbrance and the sin which so easily entangles us, and let us run with endurance the race that is set before us, 2 fixing our eyes on Jesus, the author and perfecter of faith, who for the joy set before Him endured the cross, despising the shame, and has sat down at the right hand of the throne of God."

--
[208] **2 Corinthians 3:18**
[209] **James 1:23-25**
[210] **Romans 8:15**

--

---

[211] **Romans 8:5-17**

"For those who are according to the flesh set their minds on the things of the flesh, but those who are according to the Spirit, the things of the Spirit. For the mind set on the flesh is death, but the mind set on the Spirit is life and peace, because the mind set on the flesh is hostile toward God; for it does not subject itself to the law of God, for it is not even able [to do so], and those who are in the flesh cannot please God. However, you are not in the flesh but in the Spirit, if indeed the Spirit of God dwells in you. But if anyone does not have the Spirit of Christ, he does not belong to Him. If Christ is in you, though the body is dead because of sin, yet the spirit is alive because of righteousness. But if the Spirit of Him who raised Jesus from the dead dwells in you, He who raised Christ Jesus from the dead will also give life to your mortal bodies through His Spirit who dwells in you. So then, brethren, we are under obligation, not to the flesh, to live according to the flesh-- for if you are living according to the flesh, you must die; but if by the Spirit you are putting to death the deeds of the body, you will live. For all who are being led by the Spirit of God, these are sons of God. For you have not received a spirit of slavery leading to fear again, but you have received a spirit of adoption as sons by which we cry out, "Abba! Father!" The Spirit Himself testifies with our spirit that we are children of God, and if children, heirs also, heirs of God and fellow heirs with Christ, if indeed we suffer with [Him] so that we may also be glorified with [Him]."

--

[212] **Matthew 3:13-17**

"13 Then Jesus arrived from Galilee at the Jordan [coming] to John, to be baptized by him. 14 But John tried to prevent Him, saying, 'I have need to be baptized by You, and do You come to me?' 15 But Jesus answering said to him, 'Permit [it] at this time; for in this way it is fitting for us to fulfill all righteousness.' Then he permitted Him. 16 After being baptized, Jesus came up immediately from the water; and behold, the heavens were opened, and he saw the Spirit of God descending as a dove [and] lighting on Him, 17and behold, a voice out of the heavens said, 'This is My beloved Son, in whom I am well-pleased.'

--

[213] **Matthew 3:11**

"As for me, I baptize you with water for repentance, but He who is coming after me is mightier than I, and I am not fit to remove His sandals; He will baptize you with the Holy Spirit and fire."

--

[214] **Romans 6:3-6**

[215] **Colossians 2:9-12**

--

---

[216] The New Testament Greek Lexicon uses this example:
The clearest example that shows the meaning of baptizo is a text from the Greek poet and physician Nicander, who lived about 200 B.C. It is a recipe for making pickles and is helpful because it uses both words. Nicander says that in order to make a pickle, the vegetable should first be 'dipped' (bapto) into boiling water and then 'baptized' (baptizo) in the vinegar solution. Both verbs concern the immersing of vegetables in a solution. But the first is temporary. The second, the act of baptizing the vegetable, produces a permanent change. When used in the New Testament, this word more often refers to our union and identification with Christ than to our water baptism. e.g. Mark 16:16. *"He that believes and is baptized shall be saved."* Christ is saying that mere intellectual assent is not enough. There must be a union with Him, a real change, like the vegetable to the pickle!

Thayer and Smith. "Greek Lexicon entry for Baptizo". "The NAS New Testament Greek Lexicon". . 1999. Public Domain.
Go to: http://www.biblestudytools.com/lexicons/greek/nas/baptizo.html
--

[217] **Ephesians 4:4-6**
[218] **1 Corinthians 12:13**
[219] **1 Peter 3.21**
[220] **Hebrews 12:2**
[221] **2 Corinthians 3:18**
[222] **Colossians 3:3**
[223] **1 Peter 3:18**
[224] **John 17:3**
[225] **John 17:21**
[226] **Acts 13:22**
[227] **Acts 2:1**

--
[228] **1 Corinthians 12:4-13**
"4 Now there are varieties of gifts, but the same Spirit. 5 And there are varieties of ministries, and the same Lord. 6 There are varieties of effects, but the same God who works all things in all persons. 7 But to each one is given the manifestation of the Spirit for the common good. 8 For to one is given the word of wisdom through the Spirit, and to another the word of knowledge according to the same Spirit; 9 to another faith by the same Spirit, and to another gifts of healing by the one Spirit, 10 and to another the effecting of miracles, and to another prophecy, and to another the distinguishing of spirits, to another various kinds of tongues,

and to another the interpretation of tongues. 11 But one and the same Spirit works all these things, distributing to each one individually just as He wills."

"12 For even as the body is one and yet has many members, and all the members of the body, though they are many, are one body, so also is Christ. 13 For by one Spirit we were all_baptized into one body, whether Jews or Greeks, whether slaves or free, and we were all made to drink of one Spirit."

--

[229] **John 3:13**

[230] **Colossians 2:16-17**

[231] **Hebrews 11:1 (NKJV)**

--

[232] **Hebrews 11:1b (The Mirror Bible)**

(The shadow can no longer substitute the substance. Jesus is the substance of things hoped for the evidence of everything the prophets foretold. The unveiling of Christ in human life completes man's every expectation. Col 1:27.)

--

[233] **James 2:20 (NKJV)**

[234] **James (The Mirror Bible) 2:20**

--

[235] **Colossians 1:15**

"He is the image of the invisible God, the firstborn of all creation. "

--

[236] **Colossians 2:9**

"For in Him all the fullness of Deity dwells in bodily form, . . . "

--

[237] **Proverbs 2:6**

[238] **James 1:5-6**

[239] **Hebrews 4:1-12 (HCSB)**

[240] **Philippians 4:6-7 (The Message)**

[241] **Psalms 118:24**

--

[242] **Matthew 6:19-34 (The Message)**

"Don't hoard treasure down here where it gets eaten by moths and corroded by rust or--worse!--stolen by burglars. Stockpile treasure in heaven, where it's safe from moth and rust and burglars. It's obvious,

isn't it? The place where your treasure is, is the place you will most want to be, and end up being."
(...)
"You can't worship two gods at once. Loving one god, you'll end up hating the other. Adoration of one feeds contempt for the other. You can't worship God and Money both."
*"If you decide for God, living a life of God-worship, it follows that you don't fuss about what's on the table at mealtimes or whether the clothes in your closet are in fashion. There is far more to your life than the food you put in your stomach, more to your outer appearance than the clothes you hang on your body. Look at the birds, free and unfettered, not tied down to a job description, careless in the care of God. And you count far more to him than birds."*Matthew 6:19-34 (The Message) Cont'd. - *"Has anyone by fussing in front of the mirror ever gotten taller by so much as an inch? All this time and money wasted on fashion--do you think it makes that much difference? Instead of looking at the fashions, walk out into the fields and look at the wildflowers. They never primp or shop, but have you ever seen color and design quite like it? The ten best-dressed men and women in the country look shabby alongside them."*
"If God gives such attention to the appearance of wildflowers--most of which are never even seen--don't you think he'll attend to you, take pride in you, do his best for you? What I'm trying to do here is to get you to relax, to not be so preoccupied with getting, so you can respond to God's giving. People who don't know God and the way he works fuss over these things, but you know both God and how he works. Steep your life in God-reality, God-initiative, God-provisions. Don't worry about missing out. You'll find all your everyday human concerns will be met.""Give your entire attention to what God is doing right now, and don't get worked up about what may or may not happen tomorrow. God will help you deal with whatever hard things come up when the time comes."

[243] **Isaiah 9:6**

"For a child will be born to us, a son will be given to us; And the government will rest on His shoulders; And His name will be called Wonderful Counselor, Mighty God, Eternal Father, Prince of Peace."

--

[244] **John 14:1**

"Do not let your heart be troubled; believe in God, believe also in Me."

--

[245] **John 14:27**

"Peace I leave with you; My peace I give to you; not as the world gives do I give to you. Do not let your heart be troubled, nor let it be fearful."

--

[246] **Isaiah 26:3 (NKJ)**

--

---

[247] **Psalms 91**

"1 He who dwells in the shelter of the Most High Will abide in the shadow of the Almighty. 2 I will say to the LORD, 'My refuge and my fortress, My God, in whom I trust!' 3 For it is He who delivers you from the snare of the trapper And from the deadly pestilence. 4 He will cover you with His pinions, And under His wings you may seek refuge; His faithfulness is a shield and bulwark. 5 You will not be afraid of the terror by night, Or of the arrow that flies by day; 6 Of the pestilence that stalks in darkness, Or of the destruction that lays waste at noon.7 A thousand may fall at your side And ten thousand at your right hand, [But] it shall not approach you. 8 You will only look on with your eyes And see the recompense of the wicked. 9 For you have made the LORD, my refuge, [Even] the Most High, your dwelling place.10 No evil will befall you, Nor will any plague come near your tent. 11 For He will give His angels charge concerning you, To guard you in all your ways. 12 They will bear you up in their hands, That you do not strike your foot against a stone. 13 You will tread upon the lion and cobra, The young lion and the serpent you will trample down. 14 'Because he has loved Me, therefore I will deliver him; I will set him [securely] on high, because he has known My name.' 15 'He will call upon Me, and I will answer him; I will be with him in trouble; I will rescue him and honor him.16 With a long life I will satisfy him And let him see My salvation.' "

--

[248] **Psalms 18:1-3**

[249] **Genesis 16**

--

[250] **Mark 2:27-28**

"27 Jesus said to them, 'The Sabbath was made for man, and not man for the Sabbath.' 28 'So the Son of Man is Lord even of the Sabbath.' "

--

[251] Read Exodus 33 and 34

of note Ch 33 v 14 And God said, *"My presence shall go with you, and I will give you rest."*

--

[252] **Hebrews 4:11**

--

[253] **Romans 14:17**

"For God's kingdom does not consist of food and drink, but of righteousness, peace, and joy produced by the Holy Spirit."

Printed in Australia
AUOC01n1015060416
275011AU00003B/3/P

9 780994 551108